D0177663

THE ULTIMATE RECIPE BOOK

50 CLASSIC DISHES AND THE STORIES BEHIND THEM

Angela Nilsen

THE ULTIMATE RECIPE BOOK

50 CLASSIC DISHES AND THE STORIES BEHIND THEM

Photography by Simon Wheeler

1 3 5 7 9 10 8 6 4 2

Published in 2007 by BBC Books, an imprint of Ebury Publishing.
Ebury Publishing is a division of the Random House Group Limited.

The Random House Group Limited Reg. No. 954009
Addresses for companies within the Random House Group can be found at
www.randomhouse.co.uk

A CIP catalogue record for this book is available from the British Library.

The Random House Group Limited makes every effort to ensure that the papers used
in our books are made from trees that have been legally sourced from well-managed
and credibly certified forests. Our paper procurement policy can be found at
www.randomhouse.co.uk

Set in Bembo and Helvetica Neue
Printed and bound in China by C & C Offset Printing Co. Ltd
Colour separations by Dot Gradations Ltd, UK

ISBN 978 0 563 52297 3

Commissioning Editor: Vivien Bowler Project Editor: Deirdre O'Reilly
Designer: Nigel Soper Production Controller: Peter Hunt

Please see page 186 for useful information on the recipes, including notes on ingredients, oven temperatures, spoon measurements and weight and liquid conversions.

Dedication

To Orlando Murrin – for his inspiration
and encouragement and for coming
up with the idea of creating
'Ultimate' recipes in the first place.

Contents

Foreword

Sharing food is one of the greatest acts of love we show for one another. Sharing recipes is another form of showing love for other people, as it enables us to communicate our passions and our own tastes, while imparting the precious gift of knowledge as well. Like most cooks, I got my first inspiration, and my love of eating and cooking, from one of the people who was most important to me – my mother. It is this first experience that connects food with love, which gives eating and cooking its great emotional power.

But in addition to feelings, it is important to cultivate and share skills and knowledge, and that's where cookery books come in. No good cookery book has ever been written without passion, but expertise is important too and, unlike sentiments, which can only be expressed implicitly, techniques and skills are something that can be taught by books.

Angela Nilsen has asked many chefs and food writers for their tips and advice in order to refine and hone classic recipes so that they can be used by cooks of varying abilities. The people she has asked for help have shown the generosity of spirit that is characteristic of every good cook. We all enjoy seeing people relish the food we have prepared: after all, cooking is the only art that produces something designed to be consumed. So when somebody takes pleasure in a dish we have taken trouble to make for them, they are paying us a big compliment, and we feel fulfilled too.

Angela has written the fifty recipes for classic dishes she's researched and collected in such a way as to bolster the confidence of anybody attempting them. She's tried to pass on to her readers the inspiration she's taken from the chefs and writers who have passed on their knowledge to her. While many, if not all, of these dishes will be in the repertory of most good cooks, they are recipes that almost every cook will want to master at some time or another, whether it's the fluffiest omelette or the crispest roast potatoes, the perfect chocolate sauce, or the most savoury fish cakes.

The tricks chefs use in their professional kitchens have been brought to bear on all these, and Angela has translated our unique tips into practical advice for the home cook. Before interviewing the professionals, she's compared many, many versions of each recipe, and assessed the merits and demerits of each one. She's looked at the traditional recipes and then she's looked at the modifications suggested in a huge selection of published cookbooks. She's given tips about shopping, suggested variations in ingredients, even tried to find exactly the right equipment for making each dish. Not only that, but she's also gone into the story behind the dishes. This can be important. Is macaroni cheese an Italian dish? Of course not – it's quintessentially British (or American), which makes a big difference when you think about the ingredients that go into it. It's touches like these that make *The Ultimate Recipe Book* worthy of a place on everyone's kitchen bookshelf.

RAYMOND BLANC

Introduction

I have to admit, when it was first suggested I write a feature called 'The Ultimate' for *BBC Good Food Magazine*, I wondered whether I had been handed the short straw. I was Food Editor at the time, and Orlando Murrin (then the Editor of *Good Food*) came up with the idea as a title for a new series. The concept was simple: take a classic dish, consider the way it is made, then test, modify and fine-tune all the different possibilities to create the ultimate version. Next, write up the recipe and a story to explain its development. Orlando said I should be prepared to test each recipe not once, not twice, but possibly a dozen times, whatever it took to achieve the best. My initial reaction was that studying each recipe in such detail sounded obsessive but, as I began to work on the first one, lemon tart, I was immediately fascinated and completely hooked by the whole process.

Well-known recipes I had previously taken for granted took on new meaning and stature. Taking time to delve, question, even break a few rules, meant I was no longer making these classic dishes the way I always had, out of habit. I was discovering ways to improve and update, to make them more practical and foolproof, resulting in recipes that were far better than any I had ever made before. Each Ultimate search became a culinary voyage. At the start I usually felt daunted by the endless possibilities, halfway through wondered whether I'd make it then, by the end, elated at the way the recipe turned out.

It was early on in the series that I sought the opinions of chefs and other food writers. Their expertise, tips and views helped me focus, and enlivened each story that explained the journey I took. This sharing of ideas proved inspirational, whether it was a lively conversation with Marguerite Patten about how to make the lightest scones, a serious discussion with Bill Granger on scrambling eggs, a friendly debate with Anne Willan and the chef at Claridge's over the best way to get a Yorkshire pudding to rise,

or a personal lesson from Raymond Blanc on omelette making. Invariably these interactions resulted in my having a total rethink of the recipe I was working on, and often it was some magical tip I discovered along the way, while testing, researching or chatting to the experts, that would initiate last-minute revelations. While looking for a way to stop apple slices leaking too many juices for the apple pie recipe, for example, I tried a tip from Gordon Ramsay of allowing the slices to sit and turn brown. This was the complete opposite of what I had been doing – dousing them with lemon juice to stop them discolouring – and it drew out the moisture, concentrated the flavour and solved the problem.

Whether testing the recipes in the *Good Food* kitchen or in my own kitchen, I have never been short of willing tasters. Their critical comments have all been vital in my decision-making processes, along with those of food writer Val Barrett who has been an invaluable colleague during much of the testing. When tarts cracked, meringues weeped, flapjacks fell apart, roast potatoes refused to crisp and hollandaise sauce curdled, I really didn't mind. It's what happens, and it all helped me understand and work out a better way to make each recipe. Disastrous mistakes could turn into chance discoveries, like the time I nearly burnt the syrup for summer pudding while chatting on the telephone, which resulted in the richest, jammiest fruit syrup I have ever made.

This book is an expansion of 'The Ultimate' series from *BBC Good Food Magazine*, from that very first recipe for lemon tart to all the new Ultimates that have been specially created, such as fish pie, blueberry muffins, sticky toffee pudding and salade Niçoise. I am sure there are lots more recipes just waiting to be given the Ultimate treatment, so there will be many more culinary journeys to take and share.

ANGELA NILSEN

1

ENTERTAINING MASTERPIECES

Risotto Primavera

Say the word 'risotto' to an Italian and then stand well back for a passionate response. Translated, it means 'cooked rice', but there is so much more to it, as my three risotto advisers were eager to convey. Gennaro Contaldo, chef and owner of London's Passione restaurant, exclaimed that 'amore' was what you needed to make risotto. Teacher and food writer Ursula Ferrigno spoke of 'teasing' and 'caressing' the rice, while Valentina Harris, who has written books on the subject, described risotto as 'sex on a plate'. In order to achieve the ultimate version, all three encouraged me to communicate with the rice, nurture it and enjoy taking time to make this springtime – or *primavera* – classic.

Lots to agree about

As Gennaro, Ursula and Valentina showed me their ultimate versions, I was struck by how many things they agreed on, the first being consistency. 'Creamy' was the word they all used – adding that a risotto should never be stiff and starchy. Ursula described it as being 'all'onda' – wonderfully fluid, 'like the waves in the sea,' and Gennaro as 'creamy porridge'. As to choosing the vegetables, they agreed on peas, broad beans and asparagus, with the option of a little carrot, even artichoke heart. Then there was the pan. 'It should be broad and heavy,' Ursula said. 'There's not enough room for the rice to breathe in an ordinary pan, so it's harder for it to expand and be creamy.' Being realistic, we use what we have, but Ursula's favourite is a wok-shaped pan. Also, everyone was adamant that the quality of the stock was paramount. Valentina remarked that the rice absorbs about four times its weight in liquid, and rice being bland, the liquid plays a major role in providing flavour. Once I began testing I had to agree, and the one made with homemade chicken stock had the most flavour. For vegetarians, my homemade vegetable stock version was more subtle, so I boosted the flavour with a sprinkling of vegetable bouillon powder. If you haven't got time to make your own stock, choose a good-quality powder such as Marigold Swiss or Kallo organic cubes. Whichever stock you use, 'it should be tasty enough to drink', said Valentina.

Choosing the rice

Back in my own kitchen, I still had decisions to make, especially about rice. Italy has many risotto varieties, but in the UK, our best choice is between Arborio, Carnaroli and Vialone nano. Ursula used Vialone nano, a slightly smaller, harder grain often associated with seafood by the Venetians, while Gennaro went for the softer grain Arborio, although

he agreed it is easy to overcook. Which is why Valentina suggested that Arborio is not for beginners and chose Carnaroli, explaining: 'It is the easiest to cook and get right.' I opted for Carnaroli too, being swayed by its generous size and the ease with which the creaminess was produced. However, to be honest they all make a great risotto, so I leave it to you to experiment.

1 Add the stock a ladleful at a time.

Bumping up the flavour

As with the stock, I wanted to get as much flavour into the initial fry without overpowering the delicate spring vegetables. Valentina and Ursula started with a base of finely chopped shallots, with the option of a little garlic. They then let the spring vegetables cook in the rice. Gennaro, however, introduced the idea of making a 'soffrito', a little vegetable stew, by chopping up all the veg and frying them together at the beginning. I loved the flavour this gave, but missed the freshness that the young vegetables have when they are added later. For my flavour boost, I tried an initial fry with shallots, a few spring onions (Gennaro's suggestion) and a hint of garlic. Italian cooks don't traditionally combine too many members of the onion family at this point, but a fine-tuned combination provided a lovely backdrop flavour. I now needed to address the asparagus. Unlike the peas and beans, it was taking too long to cook just in the rice and was losing its vibrancy. By dropping it briefly into the simmering stock towards the end, I added flavour without overcooking it. As to the wine, 'Never add one you wouldn't want to drink', Ursula recommended. When too much was added, however, the risotto tasted acidic.

2 Add more stock when a clear line appears after you pull a spoon across the bottom of the pan.

A steady stir

With all this advice, I was now in tune with the rice and mindful of its needs. I never left its side as it cooked, stirring it constantly to keep it creamy. 'The rice is being forced to absorb the liquid, so you must listen and watch, so it does it at its own pace rather than yours,' said Valentina. Ursula warned against adding too much stock in one go. 'If you do, all the starch comes out together. You need to tease it out gradually to get the right creaminess.' Adding a ladleful at a time worked best. Another good tip is to keep the stock simmering, ready to add, as it is more quickly absorbed than when added cold.

3 Finish with butter and Parmesan.

Serving it up

Even at the end of cooking, the rice still demanded attention. Feeding it with Parmesan and butter gave a lovely richness, and Gennaro suggested letting it rest for a few minutes while your guests gather at the table. This made the risotto even creamier. As I ladled out my final test and it settled in gentle waves on the plate, I knew the three people I had to thank for enabling me to derive so much pleasure from making this very sensual dish.

The recipe

Serves 4

Ready in just over an hour (includes skinning the beans – well worth the time)

Easy

What you need

- 200g/8oz shelled broad beans (800g/1lb 12oz in the pod)
- 4 medium shallots
- 3 spring onions, trimmed
- 1 small garlic clove
- 250g bunch asparagus
- 1.3 litres/2¼ pints good quality chicken or vegetable stock, preferably homemade
- 1 tbsp olive oil
- 85g/3oz butter
- 350g/12oz Carnaroli rice (or Arborio or Vialone nano)
- 100ml/3½fl oz dry white wine
- 140g/5oz shelled peas (450g/1lb in the pod)
- 100g/4oz Parmesan, finely grated

1. If using fresh broad beans, drop them into boiling water, leave for 1 minute, then drain and cool under cold water. Peel off the skins. For frozen beans, just thaw, then peel. Chop the shallots, spring onions and garlic as finely as you possibly can. Snap the woody bases from the asparagus spears and discard. Slice each spear into 4 diagonal pieces. Pour the stock into a separate pan and bring to a simmer.
2. Heat the oil and half the butter in a heavy, wide pan. Tip in the shallots, spring onions and garlic and cook for 3–4 minutes until soft and translucent, but not brown, stirring often. With the heat on medium, add the rice and keep it moving with a wooden spoon for a few minutes so it gets toasted, but not coloured, and very hot. Once it starts to hiss and sizzle, pour in the wine. Keep stirring for about a minute until the wine has evaporated.
3. Put the timer on for 20 minutes (it takes 18–20 minutes to add the stock), now add 1½ ladles of stock, letting it simmer, not boil. Keep stirring until all the liquid is absorbed, scraping the sides of the pan to catch any stray bits of rice. Continue to stir and add a ladleful of stock once the previous amount has been absorbed. (If you add too much stock at a time the risotto won't be as creamy.) The rice tells you when it needs more stock. You will hear it sigh and when you pull a spoon across the bottom of the pan it should leave a clear line.
4. After 14 minutes add the beans and peas to the rice with some seasoning. At the same time, drop the asparagus into the stock and let it simmer for 4 minutes, then lift out with a slotted spoon and add to the rice. Start tasting the rice now too – when done it should be softened, but with a bit of bite in the centre, almost chewy, and the risotto creamy – overcooking just makes it mushy. Continue adding stock and stirring until done (you may have a little stock left). Take the pan off the heat, add half the Parmesan and the rest of the butter plus a splash of stock to keep everything moist. Put the lid on the pan and leave for 3 minutes to rest. Serve with the remaining Parmesan.

Fish Cakes

There can't be many people who don't enjoy a well-made fish cake. At its best, it is golden and crisp on the outside, bursting with flavour and contrasting texture inside. However, fish cakes are often the opposite so, in my search for the ultimate, I sought a few expert opinions. 'The classic British fish cake is a balance between flavour and economy,' said Rick Stein. 'It's family eating, designed to make fish go a long way. The ultimate is a balance between the potato and fish, and you do want definite pieces of fish in there.' Michael Caines, executive chef at Gidleigh Park, Devon, spoke of getting 'an explosion of flavour with a light and fluffy texture. It should be a meal in itself.' Joyce Molyneux, former owner of The Carved Angel restaurant in Dartmouth, said, 'I like a large proportion of fish, well seasoned with lemon rind and herbs, so when you break into them with a fork you get a lovely herby, lemony smell.' She wasn't in favour of the oversized ones. 'They're just a little too daunting.' Food writer Diana Henry enjoys a rustic look, again not too big, 'with a good fishy experience so the potato is merely a binding.' I now had a clear idea of what I wanted to achieve. Firstly, flavour: lots of it, but I hadn't yet decided whether to use smoked fish or not. Secondly, texture: getting the mash right would be paramount (too wet and the cakes would be soggy and fall apart), and having eaten too many bland fish cakes in restaurants, I definitely wanted to know the fish was there. Then there was the choice of coating and the size: not too huge (it affects how they cook), but generous enough to be a meal in itself.

The right fish

I decided against using salmon, eager to bring flavour and texture to the classic white fish version. Thinking that smoked fish would provide an instant flavour solution, I made up a batch using just smoked haddock. Unfortunately, that's all I could taste – smoke. It was overpowering. Mixing smoked and unsmoked fish was much better, but I still felt the smokiness detracted. I would prefer other flavours to come through and balance with the fish, such as lemon and herbs. Rick Stein had said, 'This is one of those occasions when you could use one of the less overfished species, such as pollock. But Icelandic cod is really nice, too.' I switched to that and found that gentle poaching kept it soft and moist.

Marvellous mash

I wanted the potato to do two jobs: bind the fish as well as offer a flavoursome base. A floury variety gave the lightest, fluffiest mash but how best to cook it? If boiled, the potatoes were easily overcooked and became

waterlogged. 'The drier the potato is to start with the easier it is to use – you could try baking it like a jacket potato,' said Michael Caines. The potato was certainly dry done this way but it took too long. 'I sometimes boil them in their skins, then mash,' said Diana Henry. This worked well, but again, took a long time to cook. I reverted to the quicker method of boiling the potatoes and followed Rick Stein's suggestion, 'Cook the potatoes just as you do for mash. Once boiled, leave them in the colander so all the steam goes and they dry out.' To ensure thorough dryness, I also put them back in the pan and mashed them over a very low heat. As I added a knob of butter (milk only made it wet again), I wondered how I could inject more flavour. I had already tried adding flavourings such as fried onions, spring onions, anchovy essence and tarragon, but they overcomplicated it. Rick Stein had told me how he loved homemade tartare sauce with anything fried. So I came up with a quick tartare-type sauce, added a dollop to the mash instead of butter, and kept the rest to serve separately. It gave instant creaminess as well as flavour. To bring out the taste, I stirred in some chives and parsley and a little lemon zest.

1 Gently mix the flaked fish and potatoes together.

Keeping them together

One of the problems with fish cakes is that they can fall apart. Diana Henry agreed. 'They are incredibly delicate. But the more difficult they are to handle, the lighter they are and the better they taste,' she said. I had started out with the proportion of half potato to half fish, but they didn't taste fishy enough. I reduced the potato slightly (leaving enough to bind) and kept the fish chunks big so that there was no doubting their presence. A very light mixing technique was needed, especially as I didn't want the potato and fish to merge into one texture. If I used my hand to mix very briefly, the fish chunks didn't break up, and I could gently encourage the potato to bind it all together. The mixture proved easier to handle and stayed together if the fish and potato were cooled first. Also, chilling the cakes gave them firmness in readiness for frying.

2 With floured hands, carefully shape the mixture into cakes.

The final coating

To coat the cakes, the contest was between a breadcrumb finish or a dusting of flour. The crunch of the egg and breadcrumb against the softer inside made it the clear winner. With everything on the inside and outside now in harmony, I recalled something Rick Stein had said. 'Fish cakes can be on the bland side. So, it's one of those occasions where tomato ketchup is *de rigueur*.' I really hope with this recipe, however, that the idea of reaching for the ketchup bottle won't even enter your head.

3 Coat each cake with beaten egg.

The recipe

Makes 4 (easily doubled)

Ready in 50–55 minutes

Fairly easy

What you need

For the tartare-style sauce

125ml/4fl oz mayonnaise
1 rounded tbsp capers (rinsed and drained if salted), roughly chopped
1 rounded tsp creamed horseradish
1 rounded tsp Dijon mustard
1 small shallot, very finely chopped
1 tsp finely chopped fresh flat-leaf parsley

For the fish cakes

450g/1lb skinless Icelandic cod or haddock fillet, from a sustainable source
2 bay leaves
150ml/¼ pint milk
350g/12oz floury potatoes such as Maris Piper
½ tsp finely grated lemon zest
1 tbsp chopped fresh flat-leaf parsley
1 tbsp snipped fresh chives
1 egg
flour, for shaping
85g/3oz fresh white breadcrumbs, preferably a day or two old
3–4 tbsp vegetable or sunflower oil, for shallow frying
lemon wedges and watercress, to serve

Can be frozen (preferably unfried, thaw for 4 hours)

1 Mix all the sauce ingredients together. Set aside. Lay the fish and bay leaves in a frying pan. Pour over the milk and 150ml/¼ pint of water. Cover, bring to a boil, then lower the heat and simmer for 4 minutes. Take off the heat and allow to stand, covered, for 10 minutes to gently finish cooking the fish.

2 Meanwhile, peel and chop the potatoes into even-sized chunks. Put them in a saucepan and just cover with boiling water. Add a pinch of salt, bring back to the boil and simmer for 10 minutes or until tender, but not broken up.

3 Lift the fish out of the milk with a slotted spoon and put on a plate to cool. Drain the potatoes in a colander and leave for a minute or two. Tip them back into the hot pan on the lowest heat you can and let them dry out for 1 minute, mashing them with a fork and stirring so they don't stick. You should then have a light, dry fluffy mash. Take off the heat and beat in 1 rounded tablespoon of the sauce, then the lemon zest, parsley and chives. Season well with salt and pepper. The potato should have a good flavour, so taste and adjust to suit.

4 Drain off the liquid from the fish, grind some pepper over it, then flake it into big chunks into the pan of potatoes. Using your hands, gently lift the fish and potatoes together so they just mix. You'll only need a couple of turns, or the fish will break up too much. Put to one side and cool.

5 Beat the egg on a large plate and lightly flour a board. Spread the breadcrumbs on a baking sheet. Divide the fish cake mixture into four. On the floured board, and with floured hands, carefully shape into four cakes, about 2.5cm/1in thick. One by one, sit each cake in the egg, and brush over the top and sides so it is completely coated. Sit the cakes on the crumbs, patting the crumbs on the sides and tops so they are lightly covered. Transfer to a plate, cover and chill for 30 minutes (or up to a day ahead).

6 Heat the oil in a large frying pan. To test when ready, drop some of the dry breadcrumbs in – if they sizzle and quickly turn golden brown, it is ready to use. Fry the fish cakes over a medium heat for about 5 minutes on each side or until crisp and golden. Serve with the rest of the sauce (squeeze in a little lemon juice to taste), lemon wedges for squeezing over and watercress.

Steak

I've always thought that if you can master the art of cooking the perfect steak, you'll always be able to serve something special at a moment's notice. Knowing how personal the cut and cooking style of steaks can be, I asked some chefs for their views. Chef Shaun Hill advised that the choice of cut was determined by how you like to eat it. 'If you like well-done you want it crisp on the outside, but not dry on the inside, so a muscular, thinner cut is better such as rump or sirloin. Cooking a fillet to well done is a waste of money.' Marcus Wareing, head chef at Petrus in London said, 'for me it would be rib-eye with lots of marbling, but for my wife Jane I'd have to get a fillet as there is no fat or sinew, just pure meat. And it would be as rare as possible, but then not for rib-eye as the fat wouldn't get cooked enough.' Chef and restaurateur Regis Crepy told me to use sirloin, T-bone or fillet, adding, 'use quality meat from a reliable butcher. It's difficult to do something good if the quality is bad.'

Expert cooking tips

I decided that my ultimate would be a rare or medium-rare fillet steak – lightly crisp on the outside, tender as butter inside. But how to achieve it? Shaun and Regis suggested the option of flash-frying the meat in the pan, then finishing it off in the oven. However, I found I had more cooking control if I fried it on the hob. It also cooked through better when I followed Marcus's advice. 'Bring the meat out of the fridge half an hour before cooking. This takes the chill off it, otherwise it might be stone cold in the middle when done.' Wanting the flavour of butter as the steak cooked, I melted some in the pan. But as the heat needed to be high, it quickly burnt. Shaun Hill advised, 'I always use olive oil and brush it on the steak rather than heat it first in the pan. Otherwise, by the time the pan is hot enough to seal the steak, the oil will have burnt.' This worked much better, but I missed the butteriness, and remembered that Marcus drops butter in towards the end of cooking. I ended up using a combination of oil to sear the meat without burning, then butter later to colour and flavour.

When is it done?

I wanted a foolproof way to tell when the meat was cooked, but the chefs were reluctant to offer timings – too many variables, they said: thickness of the meat, cooking temperature, type of pan (a thin one loses heat more quickly, so the meat needs longer cooking). 'You can't give timings', Regis said decisively, 'you can tell by touching it.' This required experience, Shaun advised. He explained that the steak should feel soft when cooked rare, then, as the softness disappears, it becomes medium-rare and, when the middle feels like a hard rubber ball, it is well done. I found a combination of timing and touching worked best for me. Resting the steak for 5 minutes improved the texture. 'You don't want it to be shell-shocked,' said Shaun, 'which it would be if served straight from the pan into your mouth.' Resting gave the muscles time to relax after cooking, adding to the meat's tenderness. It also gave me time to whip up a quick creamy sauce – now I had something extra special.

The recipe

Serves 2

Ready in about 15 minutes

Easy

What you need

2 fillet steaks, each just over 2.5cm/1in thick
olive oil for brushing
knob of butter

1 Take the steaks out of the fridge about 30 minutes before you are ready to start cooking. (If making the sauce, see below, get these ingredients ready too.) After the steaks have lost their chill, massage a little oil all over each one and season with a little salt and plenty of pepper.
2 Heat a heavy-based frying pan to very hot. If you hold your hand a few inches above the surface of the pan, you can feel the heat coming off it when it is hot enough. Put the steaks in the pan (you will hear them sizzle), push down so they make good contact with the pan and leave them undisturbed for 1½–2 minutes for rare, or 2–2½ minutes for medium-rare. Don't be tempted to move them around. Turn and leave for another 1½–2 (for rare) or 2–2½ minutes (medium-rare) undisturbed. Just a few seconds before the end, drop in the knob of butter and as soon as it is sizzling around the steaks, take the pan off the heat. The steaks should feel soft for rare, a little firmer for medium–rare.
3 Put the steaks on a warm plate and leave to rest for 5 minutes before serving. Don't wash the pan yet if you are going to make a sauce (see below).

Mushroom-brandy sauce
Based on an idea from Marcus Wareing. While the steaks are resting you can make a quick sauce, so get any chopping and slicing done before frying the steaks. Fry 1 small chopped shallot in the butter left in the pan for about a minute until lightly coloured. Pour in 1 tablespoon brandy and let it sizzle and evaporate. Lift off the heat if necessary, then stir in a generous ½ teaspoon Dijon mustard, 6 tablespoons double cream and 50g/2oz thinly sliced button mushrooms. Leave to simmer back on the heat for a couple of minutes, then scatter in a little chopped parsley and black pepper. Pour in any meat juices that have oozed from the steaks, and serve with the steaks.

Quiche Lorraine

Halfway through working out this recipe, it struck me that what you don't put into a quiche Lorraine is as important as what you do. Over the years, quiches have become receptacles for all sorts of bits and bobs – I'm not blameless here, having got carried away on more than one occasion, throwing in salmon, watercress, brie, even broccoli, to the point where there was hardly room for the custard. But a quiche Lorraine is actually a pure dish with few ingredients – that is the real beauty of it.

Back to basics

To appreciate the original intention of this recipe, I contacted Anne Willan who runs La Varenne cooking school in France. 'There are many imposters that take the same name,' she said, 'but it only truly belongs to one dish: a flat, open tart filled with smoked, lean bacon and a combination of cream and eggs.' Food writer Marie-Pierre Moine described her ultimate version as being 'like a rich savoury custard with lots of bacon gently set in it. The custard should be creamy, not solid, and the tart slim.' Geraldene Holt, a food writer whose grandfather came from Lorraine, described her love of 'the clear, rich flavour'. She added: 'You need to go back to the beginning. It's good to revive it in its proper way.'

A case for the custard

Quiche Lorraine originated in the sixteenth century, when it was made with bread dough, not pastry. 'The French are a bit different about pastry,' said Anne Willan. 'It's not such an important part of the recipe, more a container, and rolled very thin.' She mentioned puff pastry as a possibility. However, it made the quiche very rich, so I worked on perfecting a simple, crisp pastry as a contrast to the filling. I achieved this by adding an egg yolk and extra butter. Then my concern moved to 'shrinkage'. A shallow tin gave me the slenderness I was after, but I found that if the pastry shrank even slightly, there wasn't enough room for the filling. I remembered an American trick – before baking, you trim the pastry so it sits just above the edge of the tin rather than flush with it. This was foolproof. Baking the pastry before adding the filling also proved essential, otherwise the pastry had a soggy bottom.

A light filling

Researching the recipe, I was surprised how much the filling ingredients varied. Should I use double cream, single cream, milk or a combination? Some recipes had more egg yolks than whole eggs, others between two and five whole eggs and no extra egg yolks. I found that the more

egg yolks I added, the heavier the quiche became and the more it resembled a sweet, rather than a savoury, custard. Milk had to go, too, as it couldn't provide the silky softness I sought, plus Anne told me it is widely scorned in France as a replacement for the cream. I then tested various combinations of creams and eggs – all were fine, but I knew the texture could be better. I recalled Anne's advice: 'Let the eggs play second fiddle to the cream, this assures you the best texture.' What really turned my recipe around, however, was crème fraîche thinned down with double cream. Marie-Pierre, Geraldene and Anne all spoke of its qualities – it's what the French use – and, as they explained, its acidity gives a lightness and tartness to the filling.

1 Trim the pastry edge so it sits slightly above the tin.

Simple flavour

The bacon is important, as it gives the quiche its special flavour. After various tests, I realised that it doesn't matter whether you use smoked or unsmoked – it's down to personal preference. I liked lardons (plump ribbons of bacon), but decent chopped streaky bacon was a good runner-up. I also found that if the lardons were cooked until crisp they went tough, so it was better to stop just as they started to colour. Geraldene had commented that 'crisp bacon is alien to the soft set custard', and both she and Marie-Pierre had suggested blanching the lardons before frying. It made them tender, but this was not essential to the recipe. I now wondered about introducing a bit more flavour. Anne steered me away from adding onions. 'Chives?' I enquired hesitantly. 'Oh, they will get very upset in Alsace if you do,' she replied. 'How about cheese?' I asked. This was not authentic, I was told, but just about acceptable. I grated in a little Gruyère and loved the flavour lift it gave, but it made the filling heavier. Anne explained why. 'Grated cheese just glues everything together, much better to cut it into cubes or thin slices. You want tiny pockets of cheese, not something that is going to melt and hold the custard down.'

2 Scatter the diced cheese and fried lardons over the bottom of the pastry case.

The perfect slice

I was now happy with the balance and simplicity of the filling, but getting the soft set was proving a bit hit-or-miss. When I gave the quiche a shorter cooking time, my custard filling was a perfect soft set (no longer weighed down with cheese), but far too pale on top. When baked for longer it had a lovely colour, but that soft, velvety texture disappeared and firmness set in. How could I get that rich colour without compromising the soft interior? The answer came when I adjusted the oven temperature and finely grated a little of the cheese onto the surface of the filling. As the cheese melted, it speeded up the colouring of the

3 Pour the last of the filling into the pastry case before baking.

top, so my soft set was saved. Timing was important but, as ovens vary, the look and feel of it proved more so. If I took the quiche out before it went too dark, while it still had a bit of soft bounce to it when pressed, and I cut it fresh from the oven, I knew I could anticipate that alluringly pure, gently set slice, with the little nuggets of cheese oozing over the tender bacon.

The recipe

Cuts into 8 slices

Ready in about 1¼ hours, plus 10 minutes chilling

Fairly easy

What you need
For the pastry
175g/6oz plain flour
100g/4oz cold butter, cut into pieces
1 egg yolk

For the filling
200g pack lardons, unsmoked or smoked
50g/2oz Gruyère
200ml carton crème fraîche
200ml/7fl oz double cream
3 eggs, well beaten
pinch of ground nutmeg

Can be frozen but you lose the silky texture

1 For the pastry, put the flour, butter, egg yolk and 4 teaspoons of cold water into a food processor. Using the pulse button, process until the mix binds. Tip the pastry onto a lightly floured surface, gather into a smooth ball, then roll out as thinly as you can. Line a 23cm x 2.5cm/9 x 1in loose-bottomed, fluted flan tin, easing the pastry into the base. Trim the pastry edges with scissors (save any trimmings) so it sits slightly above the tin (if it shrinks, it shouldn't now go below the level of the tin). Press the pastry into the flutes, lightly prick the base with a fork, then chill for 10 minutes. Put a baking sheet in the oven and heat to 200°C/fan 180°C/Gas 6.

2 Line the pastry base with foil, shiny side down, fill with dry beans and bake on the hot sheet for 15 minutes. Remove the foil and beans and bake for 4–5 minutes more until the pastry is pale golden. If you notice any small holes or cracks, patch up with pastry trimmings. *You can make it up to this point a day ahead.*

3 While the pastry cooks, prepare the filling. Heat a small frying pan, tip in the lardons and fry for a couple of minutes. Drain off any liquid that comes out, then continue cooking until the lardons just start to colour, but aren't crisp. Remove and drain on kitchen paper. Cut three quarters of the cheese into small dice and finely grate the rest. Scatter the diced cheese and fried lardons over the bottom of the pastry case.

4 Using a spoon, beat the crème fraîche to slacken it then slowly beat in the double cream. Mix in the beaten eggs. Season (you shouldn't need much salt) and add nutmeg. Pour three-quarters of the filling into the pastry case.

5 Half-pull the oven shelf out and put the flan tin on the baking sheet. Quickly pour the rest of the filling into the pastry case – you get it right to the top this way. Scatter the grated cheese over the top, then carefully push the shelf back into the oven. Lower the oven to 190°C/fan 170°C/Gas 5. Bake for about 25 minutes, or until golden and softly set (the centre should not feel too firm). Let the quiche settle for 4–5 minutes, then remove from the tin. Serve freshly baked, although it's also good cold.

Fish Pie

What makes the ultimate fish pie? Since opinions varied so much, I asked Rick Stein to decide. 'The classic British fish pie is with mash and lots of fish. It doesn't need modernizing, and it's time for a revival,' he told me. I agreed that mash gave the ultimate comfort-food topping, but it is also mash that has caused me problems before, as it invariably sinks into the creamy sauce below. So initially I tried pies with pastry on top, then chunks of potatoes, but these were avoidance tactics.

Flavouring the fishy layer

Putting the topping aside, I moved onto the sauce and fish. Fish pie deserves a touch of luxury so the sauce would definitely be creamy. When I fried an onion and used that as the buttery base for the béchamel sauce, its flavour was transformed, along with a little dill and nutmeg. For the fish, I tried various combinations with haddock as the base, including smoked fish (a bit strong), some scallops and lobster (a bit rich), before settling on a traditional mix of haddock and salmon with king prawns thrown in. But the consistency of the sauce still wasn't right. Not wanting to overcook the fish I added it raw to the sauce, but when the pie came out of the oven the sauce was far runnier than when it went in. I contacted chef Michael Caines. 'Don't make the sauce too thin,' he advised. 'Bear in mind that when added raw, the fish gives off some liquid.' To counteract this, and still prevent overcooking, I part-cooked the fish in milk first. The milk became part of the liquid for the sauce (which added flavour) and the fish no longer oozed liquid into it.

No more sinking mash

Back to the topping. To prevent the potato sinking, I followed Rick's tip. 'Chilling the sauce is important,' he said, 'unless you don't mind the sauce poking through the pie, that is.' Chilling gave a firmer base, but the topping and sauce still needed to work in unison. For creaminess I beat lots of butter and milk into the mash. It didn't sink, but the tasters agreed that although the sauce was just right (lots of flavour, slightly runny but not too much, with generous pieces of fish), the mash was far too soft – too similar to the sauce. I needed to keep it creamy but get it firmer, and inject more flavour. After boiling the potatoes I let them dry, kept milk to a minimum, let butter enrich, and beat in Rick's suggested additions of an egg yolk and Parmesan. With a final brushing of melted butter to glaze, the difference in texture and taste was dramatic. And yes, this pie is time-consuming, but it's perfect for entertaining. As Rick remarked, 'once it's made, you don't have to do anything.'

Make-ahead tip
The pie can be made up completely a day ahead, chilled, then reheated at the same temperature as the recipe, for 45 minutes.

The recipe

Serves 6

Ready in about 1 hour 20 minutes, plus 1 hour or overnight chilling

Fairly easy

What you need

450g/1lb skinless salmon fillet
450g/1lb skinless haddock fillet (from a sustainable source)
425ml/¾ pint full-fat milk, plus 1 tbsp
few sprigs of fresh thyme (lemon thyme is good)
1 bay leaf
284ml carton single cream
85g/3oz butter, plus extra for brushing potatoes
1 medium onion, chopped
50g/2oz plain flour, minus 1 tsp
2 rounded tbsp chopped or snipped fresh dill
⅛ tsp freshly grated nutmeg
175g/6oz cooked, shelled, king prawns
1kg/2¼ lb floury potatoes, such as Maris Piper or King Edward
1 egg yolk
25g/1oz finely grated Parmesan

Can be frozen (as long as the fish hasn't been frozen before)

1 Put the salmon and haddock in a large frying pan in a single layer, cutting to fit if necessary. Pour the 425ml/¾ pint of milk over. Wrap the thyme sprigs inside the bay leaf, tie up with string and drop into the pan. Bring to the boil then lower the heat and simmer for 4 minutes. Take the pan off the heat, cover and leave for 5 minutes to almost cook the fish. (Don't worry if the centre is slightly undercooked at this stage.) Lift the fish from the milk with a slotted spoon onto a large plate. Strain the hot milk into a saucepan. Pour in the cream and warm through but don't boil.

2 Melt 50g/2oz of the butter in a medium saucepan. Add the onion and fry for about 5 minutes until soft but not brown, stirring occasionally. Stir in the flour and cook for 1 minute, stirring. Remove from the heat and pour in one third of the hot creamy milk. Beat it really well to incorporate the roux (flour mixture). Pour in another third and beat again really well. Pour in the last third of milk and beat again. Put the pan back on the heat and cook, stirring, until thickened and smooth. Lower the heat and simmer for 4 minutes until glossy, giving it a stir every now and then. Remove from the heat and stir in the dill and nutmeg and season to taste with salt and pepper.

3 Separate the fish into very big pieces (6–7.5cm/2½–3in) removing any bones as you find them. (If too small the pieces will break up later.) Season with pepper. Lightly butter a 2–2.25 litre/3½–4 pint casserole dish and layer the fish chunks and prawns in it. Pour the sauce over, give a couple of gentle stirs to combine everything, without breaking up the fish, and chill for an hour or two (or overnight).

4 Meanwhile, peel the potatoes and cut into even-sized chunks, about 2.5–4cm/1–1½in. Put into a saucepan, cover with boiling water, bring back to the boil, add salt, then boil gently for 10 minutes until tender. Tip them into a colander to drain for a minute or so, then tip them back into the pan and put on a very low heat for no more than a minute to dry. Remove from the heat, add the remaining 25g/1oz butter and the egg yolk and beat with an electric hand whisk to mash. Add the tablespoon of milk and beat until fluffy with a wooden spoon. Stir in the Parmesan and season with salt and pepper if needed. The mash should be creamy and spreadable, but not too soft. Leave to cool slightly. Heat the oven to 200°C/fan 180°C/Gas 6.

5 Spoon the potatoes over the saucy fish so it is completely covered. Roughly fork over the surface then brush with a little melted butter. Bake for about 30 minutes until the sauce is bubbly and the potatoes tinged golden.

Roast Chicken

My search for the ultimate roast chicken had me roasting at least a dozen chickens, every which way, and I have to confess I've discovered so much, I'm going to be doing it completely differently from now on.

Choosing the chicken

There were no surprises here. How could an economy bird be better than one that had roamed freely on a natural diet? It couldn't and it wasn't. Though double the price, the free-range, organic chicken came out tops. I ordered a French Bresse chicken from a local butcher. Named after the region it is reared in, this is the *appellation contrôlée* of chickens, and well deserves this title. It even smelt good raw. However, the cost makes it a once-in-a-blue-moon treat. More affordable were the organic birds. I tried one from a butcher, and another from a supermarket and both were meltingly moist. Though we've unfortunately come to expect chicken to be a cheap meat to be eaten regularly, it became clear you get what you pay for, and I concluded that it's better to buy the best you can, and offer it the respect it deserves.

Preparing it for the oven

Have you ever struggled to follow step-by-step photos of how to truss a chicken? Don't bother. It looks neat, but I found squeezing it up like that made it difficult to cook thoroughly. The heat penetrated better when I laid the bird in a relaxed fashion in the tin, with the wings tucked under in a sunbathing position so they didn't burn. Wanting to enhance the natural flavour, rather than detract from it, I stuffed the cavity with chunks of onion, a sprig of herb and a lemon (using the Italian trick of pricking it with a skewer to release the flavour). Next dilemma: oil or butter? I contacted Valentina Harris who, being Italian, 'anoints it thoroughly with extra-virgin olive oil'. Anne Willan in France says, 'only butter will do – nothing else browns the same or gives the same flavour.' I tried both and preferred the French method for flavour and finish, the Italian for health – I'll leave that choice to you. My old method of smothering a bird in butter with my fingers was a bit cavalier. Instead I achieved an even coating by gently brushing with melted butter. After a generous sprinkling of salt and pepper, the chicken was ready for the oven. I cooked chickens high, low, high then low, low then high, but preferred the less complex way of keeping the oven at a steady 190°C. Not only was it less bother, I felt it was kinder to the meat. I found that 20 minutes per 450g/1lb was perfect, with an added extra 10 minutes or so if necessary after testing (see recipe on page 33).

Best way to roast

I've often read how turning a chicken during roasting makes it more moist, something I've always shied away from, thinking it too fiddly. How wrong I was. I began the tests by starting the bird upside down, then turning it – a really moist result but not a looker, as the breast came out all squashed. Roasting upright without turning gave a great golden glow to the skin, but the flesh wasn't as moist. The best method was to start the chicken on its side on a rack, propped up with bunched up foil to stop it toppling over, then turning it to the other side before finishing it right way up. This was well worth the effort, and it was even easier when I discovered a special V-shaped rack that supported the chicken. A rack also had the effect of elevating the bird from the base of the roasting tin, helping it to cook better. I also tried cooking the chicken on a platform of chopped onions and carrots, which made it a bit more precarious to turn, but had the added bonus of producing some delicious roast veg to serve with the meat. I debated the matter of basting throughout the testing. Anne Willan feels it is the key to getting the skin crisp, and recommends doing so every 10 minutes. I found there was little difference whether I basted methodically or just when I remembered. My final test emerged in all its glory: plump and moist, succulent and tender with a wonderful flavour and golden well-seasoned skin. Letting it relax for 10–15 minutes before carving allowed the juices to redistribute themselves, giving the best chicken I have ever roasted.

1 Prick the lemon all over to release the juices before pushing into the chicken cavity.

2 An adjustable V-shaped rack elevates the chicken and helps it to cook evenly.

3 As an added extra, add red onion, crème fraîche and some stock to make a quick gravy.

The recipe

Serves 4

Ready in 1½–1¾ hours, plus 15 minutes resting

Easy

What you need

1 lemon
1 small onion, peeled and quartered
1.6–1.8kg/3½–4lb organic chicken, the best you can afford
sprigs of bay leaves, or bunch of fresh tarragon
25g/1oz butter, and a bit extra to butter the tin
wedges of red onion and/or carrot if you don't have a rack, or 1 large red onion, peeled and cut in thick wedges, for optional gravy

1 Heat the oven to 190°C/fan oven 170°C/Gas 5. Halve the lemon and prick all over many times with a skewer or toothpick – this releases the juices and adds fragrance to the chicken as it roasts. Push the onion and lemon into the cavity of the chicken, along with the bay or tarragon. Keep the other sprigs for garnish.

2 Melt the butter in a small pan or more quickly in the microwave and brush the chicken all over with a pastry brush, including the parts where the thighs meet the body of the bird. Season liberally with salt and freshly ground pepper.

3 Now you have a choice. If you have a rack, sit the bird on that, on its side, propped up with balls of foil if the rack is flat. If not, put a few chunks of carrot, red onion or both on the bottom of a buttered roasting tin (choose one that the bird will fit into snugly) and sit the chicken on them.

4 Roast for 20 minutes on the first side. Then, if the bird is on a rack, scatter the red onion underneath if you want to make the gravy (see below). Turn, then baste with some of the juices and roast for 20 minutes on the other side. A clean tea towel makes it easier to hang on to the bird for turning. Turn the chicken breast-side up, keep the wings tucked under and baste again. Discard any foil and roast for another 30–40 minutes until really golden. To test whether the chicken is cooked, push a skewer into the fleshiest part and if the juices are clear, rather than pink, it is done. Or give the legs a bit of a tug – the chicken is done if they wiggle and move away from the body easily. If not, roast a bit longer.

5 Lift the chicken out the oven and leave it to relax, loosely covered with foil, for 10–15 minutes. Sit it on your best platter and tuck a few bay sprigs in the cavity.

Simple creamy gravy

I picked up a great tip for a quick gravy from food writer Jeni Wright. Scatter a red onion, in wedges, in the bottom of the roasting tin for the last 50 minutes. Remove the chicken from the tin and, while it rests, tip a 250g carton of crème fraîche into the tin with the onion and juices and heat through, stirring. If you want to make it go further, pour in some stock.

Lamb Biryani

As so many Indian restaurants and chefs can justifiably boast they make the best biryani, would my quest be futile? After all, it's one of India's noblest delicacies and can require much skill. I spoke with Atul Kochhar, chef and owner of Benares restaurant in London. He told me of places in India that specialize in cooking biryani, such as in Matka Peer in Delhi where people leave their cooking pots with chefs in the morning then return in the evening to collect their cooked biryanis. 'The rice and meat (classically lamb) are mixed when raw with spices and fragrances and left to smoulder slowly in sealed pots over charcoal ashes for several hours.' He didn't advise this method for me, suggesting instead, 'to make a lamb curry, add parboiled rice to it and put it in the oven.' I knew it would be more complex than that but it was a start.

The experts advise

Over the years, Lucknow, Hyderabad and Kerala have all been famed for their characteristically different biryanis from which many hybrids have evolved, Atul explained. To achieve my version, he advised that 'the grains of rice should be separate, it has to be full of flavour and moist. You can't have a dry biryani.' Meena Pathak, co-founder of Patak's Foods, has a simple version for mid-week, and a more elaborate one 'when I want to impress people,' she told me. 'The spicing should be aromatic, not hot, and the meat tender, just falling apart. I layer it up, you need to get the flavours running through.' Meena agreed that a biryani has to be moist, 'but you don't want liquid floating in it, so the amount of liquid to cook the rice in is crucial, as it gets absorbed. A biryani should be sufficient to eat as a meal in itself, with just a yogurt raita to serve.'

Many decisions to make

I began testing by experimenting with different spice combinations. Atul helped here: 'cinnamon, clove, cumin, saffron all enhance the flavour of lamb – the flavours are quite Christmassy'. I tried marinating the meat in yogurt as opposed to stirring the yogurt in at the end. Rice was cooked plain, with added spices, with different amounts and types of liquid, and by different methods. I fried the onions and puréed them with the yogurt to use as a marinade (which Atul does) and also tried layering the fried onion with the rice and meat. Decisions were made then changed as testing progressed. When the recipe reached all expectations, Atul's idea of pouring spiced butter and saffron milk over at the end kept it fragrantly moist. As I dug down through the gently spiced layers, I knew this ultimate quest had not been in vain.

Coriander and tomato raita

Based on an idea from Atul Kochhar. Briefly dry fry ½ teaspoon cumin seeds in a small pan until toasty in both aroma and appearance. Grind to a powder, then mix with 2 x 150g tubs of natural yogurt, 1 small seeded finely chopped tomato, a handful of chopped coriander and salt to taste.

The recipe

Serves 4

Ready in 3 hours, includes 1 hour marinating time

Fairly easy

What you need
150g carton natural yogurt
3 garlic cloves, grated
1 heaped tsp finely grated fresh root ginger
½ tsp ground cinnamon
¾ tsp turmeric
600g/1lb 5oz lean boneless leg of lamb, trimmed of excess fat
generous pinch of saffron strands
5 tbsp tepid milk
4 medium onions
7 tbsp vegetable oil
½ tsp hot chilli powder
280g/10oz basmati rice
1 cinnamon stick, halved
5 green cardamom pods, lightly bashed to split
4 cloves
1 tsp cumin seeds
700ml/1¼ pints chicken stock
1 tsp garam masala powder
25g/1oz butter, melted

To serve
handful of toasted almonds or cashews
1 tbsp finely chopped fresh mint leaves
1 tbsp finely chopped fresh coriander leaves
Coriander and tomato raita (see page 34)

1 Mix together the yogurt, grated garlic and ginger, cinnamon, turmeric and one teaspoon of salt in a shallow dish. Cut the lamb into pieces (about 2.5cm/1in) and stir into the yogurt mix. Leave to marinate for 1–3 hours – the longer the better. Stir the saffron into the milk and leave to dissolve.

2 After the meat has marinated, slice one of the onions in half lengthways, then cut into very thin slices. In a heavy-based wok or sauté pan, heat 2 tablespoons of the oil. Add the onion and fry over a medium heat until golden (5–8 minutes). Next add the yogurt-coated meat a tablespoon at a time, stirring and allowing it to fry briefly before you add the next spoonful. (Adding it gradually helps stop the yogurt from curdling.) When all the lamb has been added, fry for 10 minutes, stirring often, until the juices start to come out. Stir in the chilli powder and 50ml/2fl oz water. Turn the heat to low and cook, covered, on a slow simmer for 1–1¼ hours or until the meat is very tender, stirring occasionally. Tip the rice into a bowl, cover with cold water and leave to soak for 20 minutes, then drain.

3 While the meat is cooking, cook the rest of the onions. Slice them as before, very thinly. Heat 3 tablespoons of the oil in a large sauté pan, add the onions and sprinkle with a little salt (this helps to stop them from burning). It seems a lot of onions, but they reduce down. Fry over a medium heat for about 25 minutes, stirring occasionally, until evenly golden brown all over. Tip the onions onto kitchen paper and spread them out into a thin layer. Leave to cool. No need to wash the pan yet as you can use it for the rice.

4 Cook the rice. Heat the remaining 2 tablespoons of oil in the onion pan, tip in the cinnamon, cardamom, cloves and cumin seeds and fry for a minute until you start to smell the aroma. Add the rice and fry for a minute, stirring all the time. Stir in the stock and bring it to the boil. Cover and cook over a medium heat for about 8 minutes until the stock has been absorbed. Take off the heat and let the rice stand with the lid on, so it can fluff up some more. Mix the garam masala with the melted butter. Heat the oven to 180°C/fan 160°C/Gas 4.

5 Butter a 2–2.25 litre/3½–4 pint casserole dish and spoon in half the cooked lamb and any juices (a lot will have been absorbed, so you should be left with enough to coat the meat), then scatter over one third of the fried onions. Pick out the cinnamon, cloves and cardamom from the rice (they should have risen to the surface). Spoon half the rice over the lamb and onions, then pour over the spiced butter. Add another layer of lamb and another third of the onions. Finish with the rest of the rice, and drizzle the saffron milk over the top. Scatter over the rest of the onions and the toasted nuts, cover tightly with a lid or foil and put in the oven for about 20 minutes or until heated through. Sprinkle with the mint and coriander and serve with the raita.

Thai Green Chicken Curry

I felt daunted by the prospect of coming up with my own version of this recipe, especially when Ken Hom told me 'there are as many different versions of it as there are Thai cooks'. I was soon encouraged, however, when he added, 'so at the end of the day there is no right or wrong one.' Vatcharin Bhumichitr, author and restaurateur, warned me it is hard to give exact amounts as everyone's tastes are different, and as chef and author Tom Kime began to explain the intricacies of Thai cuisine, I appreciated its many complexities.

Discussions begin

All my advisers stressed the need for a good green curry base. David Thompson, author of *Thai Food* (Pavilion), said, 'the best way to ensure it is to make your own so you get an aromatic, spicy paste. I prefer using a pestle and mortar and pounding it to within an inch of its life.' Tom Kime agreed about making your own, but suggested a food processor would be an easier tool. He advised adding the ingredients in stages. 'If you put the soft and hard ingredients in all together,' he said, 'you will end up with a mush, so finely chop the hard ones first before they go in.' Both Ken Hom and Vatcharin Bhumichitr agreed that if you could find a top-quality bought curry paste, that would be good enough. For convenience I agreed, but would it do for the ultimate?

Homemade wins

I picked up an authentic-looking tub of curry paste in my local supermarket and made up the first test. When raw, the sludgy green paste smelt vaguely musty, but it enabled me to have a very acceptable green curry on the table in under half an hour. Next I gathered all the ingredients together to make my own paste, which was time consuming in itself. Chilli is vital, used like coriander as Vatcharin had told me, for colour as well as flavour. I knew I wasn't adding nearly as many chillies as Thai cooks would, but the potency of them still made itself felt. David Thompson had told me that 'in southern Thailand they throw in small chillies viciously and relentlessly. It can be insanely hot.' Tom's advice was, 'it's good to taste the chilli, but not so it blows your socks off.' He then explained the role of coriander. 'In the West we tend to throw away the root of the coriander, thinking it to be dirty and muddy – but it is vital for flavour. If you don't have roots, use the base part of the coriander stem.' All had advised that a fine paste was important. With time and patience I could get it finer using a pestle and mortar than a machine, but if I was going to the trouble of making the paste,

I preferred the ease and speed of the mixer. Pre-chopping up the harder ingredients first, such as the lemon grass, garlic and galangal, as Tom had suggested, made for a better texture. Never mind all the effort, the home-made paste had to be the winner. Its taste, colour, aroma – everything about it was fresh and vibrant.

1 Finely chop the shallots, lemon grass, garlic, galangal, and the coriander stems.

An unexpected dilemma

With the time-consuming bit done, putting the curry together should have been quick but there were complications ahead. I confirmed what I was aiming for. 'You want to create a balance of flavours of hot, sweet, salt and sour all in one mouthful,' Tom explained, 'so keep tasting and adjusting.' Vatcharin spoke of the need for balance too. 'Even with hot things like this, I like to add sugar to balance, and use fish sauce for the salty taste, like Europeans use salt.' Ken Hom spoke of having 'a savoury taste and fragrance at the same time.' Coconut is essential – but should it be coconut milk or coconut cream? David Thompson was adamant. 'Green curry almost invariably has coconut cream in,' he told me. As a purist, he would have me making it too. Instead I bought both coconut cream and milk and had a cook-off. Following Ken Hom's advice I fried the curry paste in oil first, 'you are coaxing all the flavour out and it makes it much more aromatic,' he told me. I then poured in coconut milk and dropped in the sliced raw chicken. The liquid separated out into a curdled watery mass, plus the chicken was tasteless. The raw chicken must have reacted with the liquid coconut. Vatcharin then mentioned, 'if you cook the chicken in the curry paste, the flavour will soak in.' This bumped the flavour of the chicken right up, and stabilised the sauce. However, I found that whether I used coconut cream or milk as the only liquid, the sauce was cloyingly rich.

2 Stir in 2 rounded tablespoons of the curry paste and fry, stirring.

Lighter sauce, lingering flavours

I did more research and discovered recipes suggesting I fry and reduce the coconut liquid until the oil separated out. I tried again. After frying the paste then coconut cream, I briefly cooked the chicken in this fragrant base which tenderised and flavoured it. 'The key is that it should be quite soup-like', Tom advised, 'not thick like chicken korma.' I thinned the reduced coconut with stock and ended up with a fresher, lighter sauce with a greater depth of flavour. All was now adjusted and balanced. I remembered Tom saying I would get all the flavours on different parts of my tongue – and it was true, long after I had eaten my final test they were still tingling their way around my mouth. Vatch had said 'every house in Thailand does their own version to suit their own taste.' This one certainly suits my house – I hope it suits yours too.

3 Keep stirring as the coconut cream bubbles and reduces to a thickish paste.

The recipe

Serves 4

Ready in about 50–55 minutes

Fairly easy

What you need

For the green curry paste

3 shallots, peeled
2 lemon grass stalks, ends and any tough outer layers peeled
3 plump garlic cloves
2.5cm/1in piece galangal (Thai ginger, which has a different taste to root ginger), peeled
small bunch fresh coriander (about 25g/1oz), stems and leaves separated
3 small green chillies, finely chopped
2 fat green chillies, chopped
½ tsp ground cumin
½ tsp ground coriander
2 kaffir lime leaves
1 tbsp vegetable oil

For the curry

4 skinless, boneless chicken breasts
2 tbsp vegetable oil
1 garlic clove, chopped
1 mild green chilli, finely shredded
2 x 200ml cartons coconut cream
1½ tbsp fish sauce (a lighter one has better flavour)
½ tsp light muscovado sugar
about 400ml/14fl oz chicken stock
4 kaffir lime leaves
100g/4oz snow peas, sliced lengthways into thin strips

1 To make the curry paste, finely chop the shallots, lemon grass, garlic, galangal, and the coriander stems. Put them all in a food processor and pulse until it is as smooth as it will go. Add the chillies and coriander leaves, the ground cumin and coriander, a quarter teaspoon of salt, crumble in the lime leaves then pulse until it's as smooth as you can get it, adding the oil and a tablespoon of water to help it all bind. (It's hard to get the paste completely smooth in a food processor.)

2 For the curry, cut the chicken into thin strips. Heat the 2 tablespoons of oil in a wok or deep frying pan, add the garlic and chilli and fry briefly. Before the garlic starts to brown, stir in 2 rounded tablespoons of the curry paste and fry, stirring, for just under a minute. Pour in the coconut cream, bring to a boil and with the heat medium-high, keep stirring as the cream bubbles and reduces to a thickish paste with a slight sheen, as the oil starts to separate. This takes about 8–10 minutes. Add the chicken and stir-fry for a minute so it is coated in the paste and no longer opaque. Stir in the fish sauce and sugar. Slowly pour in the stock so you have a thinnish creamy sauce. Add the lime leaves. Simmer gently for 5 minutes or until the chicken is cooked.

3 While the chicken simmers, steam the snow peas for 2 minutes. Tip them into the sauce and thin with more stock if necessary. To serve, spoon some rice into each bowl, spoon the chicken curry on top, letting the sauce fall around the rice, and pile a little shredded spring onion, ginger and a few coriander leaves onto the curry. Serve with lime wedges for squeezing over.

To serve

250g/9oz Thai fragrant rice, cooked
2 spring onions, finely shredded (see Tips below)
a few long, thin slices of fresh root ginger, peeled and finely shredded
fresh coriander leaves
lime wedges

Tips

• You use about half of the curry paste for this recipe. The rest will keep in the fridge for up to 4–5 days, or can be frozen for up to a month. It's handy to have for quickly putting a curry together. For another meat try beef or, for vegetarian, chunks of pumpkin or squash.

• To make the spring onions go curly and crisp, shred them an hour or two ahead and leave in a bowl of ice-cold water in the fridge.

2

PERFECT FOR SUPPER

Spaghetti Carbonara

Eager to discover the ultimate spaghetti carbonara, I began my research back to front. I should have gone straight to an Italian – after all, it's believed the Italians named it after the Carbonari, members of a secret society that flourished in the early 19th century who created it as a quick, filling meal. If the British had invented it, they would probably have called it egg-and-bacon pasta and left it at that. However, although my route was circuitous, it was most intriguing. The quest began by quizzing a few foodie friends. One, saying he was a purist, insisted the recipe should have only spaghetti, pancetta, egg yolks and Parmesan. Another lamented the fact that the Italians made it so much better than she did as she was always left with scrambled or burnt egg on the bottom of the pan. Some said they added whole eggs, others just the yolks. One person threw in the idea of using bucatini, a plump version of spaghetti, as is done traditionally in Lazio, and another of livening it all up with chilli flakes.

Sorting out the ingredients – first few attempts

The debate was hotting up. Presented with so much choice, I wrote out a list of the possibilities. I wanted the recipe to be as traditional as possible, the sauce was to be creamy but not swimming in cream, eggs definitely not scrambled and – the biggest challenge of all – it was to be delightfully light. I got the amount of spaghetti right early on (350g/12oz for four). Most recipes call for more, but it made everything too heavy and the texture of dried pasta worked much better than fresh. I tracked down bucatini in an Italian deli, but rejected it due to its thickness (the slender spaghetti was easier to eat). Pancetta won out over bacon, the flavour being more rounded, and butter added to the flavour, so proved better than oil for frying. I was after a hint of garlic, but the taste proved overpowering when it was fried with the pancetta. I also needed to eliminate the greasiness of the dish, find a foolproof way to stop the eggs scrambling, and still hadn't decided which cheese worked best.

Less garlic, please

To cut the greasiness, I tried eliminating the butter and let the pancetta fry alone. I got it nice and crisp by frying it long and slow. It gave off so much fat that I drained off a lot, leaving a bit in the pan for flavour and moistness. The garlic was now nicely balanced as I had squashed it, using it to flavour the pan, then taken it out. I couldn't decide on whole eggs or yolks, so in the end went with a combination, mainly for creaminess. And an equal mix of Pecorino and Parmesan tasted best.

The elusive secret of creamy eggs

This proved tricky. During my research, I had found that other cooks had struggled with the challenge of keeping everything hot without letting the eggs overcook. The most creative idea I had read was to put a dish with the beaten eggs and cheese in a very low oven so they were warm and slightly cooked when tossed with the pasta. A bit fussy, I thought, so I tried putting the hot, drained spaghetti back in its pan on a very low heat, but when the eggs were added it was hard to stop them scrambling. Pouring the eggs in off the heat meant they didn't scramble so easily and the warmth of the spaghetti was still sufficient to lightly cook them. But I had created another problem. By eliminating most of the fat, I no longer had enough sauce to coat the pasta. So I reluctantly added cream, which instantly did the trick. All seemed fine, but it did have to be eaten quickly as the pasta soon mopped up the sauce. I scattered over chopped parsley and thought I had my ultimate version, despite a nagging doubt that I had compromised by adding cream. Should I have left in the butter?

An Italian to the rescue

Then a chance meeting with chef Gennaro Contaldo prompted a complete rethink. He feels carbonara in the UK has lost its identity, 'I see it made with onion, bacon, a lot of cream, even béchamel sauce.' He offered to show me how to make his version. As he grated, chopped and fried in the compact kitchen of his restaurant, Passione, in London, he confirmed my choice of cheese, the way I added garlic flavour, the amount of pasta, but the biggest revelation was to come. His carbonara was wonderfully creamy, but not a drop of cream was added. He fried the pancetta in butter, but pasta water was the magic ingredient. It dripped in as he transferred the spaghetti to the hot frying pan. The spaghetti and pancetta were then very hot as the eggs and cheese went in, off the heat, with more pasta water splashed in from a ladle. With the butter the pancetta had been fried in, everything mingled to make a light, silky-smooth sauce, enough to coat the pasta glossily without drowning it. And with no cream, the flavour of the cheese was stronger. I had added a sprinkling of parsley to pretty up the dish and although Gennaro agreed to it, it wasn't needed. This spaghetti carbonara is beautiful in its simplicity.

1 While the spaghetti is cooking, fry the pancetta and garlic.

2 Lift the cooked spaghetti with a pasta fork and add to the pancetta.

3 Use a long-pronged fork to twist the pasta onto a plate.

The recipe

Serves 4

Ready in 25–35 minutes

Easy

What you need

100g/4oz pancetta
50g/2oz Pecorino cheese
50g/2oz Parmesan
3 eggs, preferably organic
350g/12oz spaghetti
(De Cecco is very good)
2 plump garlic cloves, peeled
and left whole
50g/2oz unsalted butter

1 Put a large saucepan of water on to boil. Finely chop the pancetta, having first removed any rind. Finely grate both cheeses and mix them together. Beat the eggs in a medium bowl, season with a little freshly ground black pepper and set everything aside.

2 Add 1 teaspoon salt to the boiling water, add the spaghetti and when the water comes back to the boil, cook at a constant simmer, covered, for 10 minutes or until *al dente* (just cooked).

3 Squash the garlic with the blade of a knife, just to bruise it. While the spaghetti is cooking, fry the pancetta with the garlic. Drop the butter into a large wide frying pan or wok and, as soon as the butter has melted, tip in the pancetta and garlic. Leave these to cook on a medium heat for about 5 minutes, stirring often, until the pancetta is golden and crisp. The garlic has now imparted its flavour, so take it out with a slotted spoon and discard.

4 Keep the heat under the pancetta on low. When the pasta is ready, lift it from the water with a pasta fork or tongs and put it in the frying pan with the pancetta. Don't worry if a little water drops in the pan as well (you want this to happen) and don't throw the rest of the pasta water away yet.

5 Mix most of the cheese in with the eggs, keeping a small handful back for sprinkling over later. Take the pan of spaghetti and pancetta off the heat. Now quickly pour in the eggs and cheese and, using the tongs or a long fork, lift up the spaghetti so it mixes easily with the egg mixture (which thickens but doesn't scramble) and everything is coated. Add extra pasta-cooking-water to keep it saucy (several tablespoons should do it). You don't want it wet, just moist. Season with a little salt, if needed.

6 Use a long-pronged fork to twist the pasta onto the serving plate or bowl. Serve immediately with a little sprinkling of the remaining cheese and a grating of black pepper. If the dish does get a little dry before serving, splash in some more hot pasta water and the glossy sauciness will be revived.

French Omelette

Learning to make an omelette is a bit like learning to dance. You need to practise a bit and feel the rhythm so you end up cooking it instinctively rather than trying to follow a recipe. Everything happens very quickly, so getting into the flow makes it easier to feel in control. Elizabeth David wrote in *French Provincial Cooking* (Penguin), 'There is only one infallible recipe for the perfect omelette: your own.'

Picking the right pan

Your pan will be crucial. Searching my cupboards for a suitable one, I realised they were all too big to make individual omelettes. So I went in search of 18–20cm pans to test. I found a cheap iron pan which worked beautifully, but was impractical as it needed seasoning regularly. So for versatility and reliability, a solid, good-quality, non-stick pan with high, slightly rounded sides won out. Your pan needn't be expensive but the better it conducts heat, the quicker the cooking. I tested mine on electric and gas, and found that regulating the heat was easier with gas.

Get the ingredients, then begin

Since eggs are the main ingredient, they should be the best, so I bought organic free-range eggs from the supermarket, and a selection of butters. But how many eggs? There's a traditional French Easter recipe for a giant omelette that uses 5,000 eggs, and needs a fork-lift truck to move the pan. However, I decided three large eggs in my pan would be fine. Two eggs made a mean omelette and four didn't cook so well. Also, I used unsalted butter as salted burnt too easily. By now omelettes were sliding out of my pan at a fast rate and the eggs were giving a lovely flavour and colour. I'd got the heat of the pan just right: the butter tells you, as it should sizzle when added. If the pan's too hot, the eggs overcook; if too cold, they take too long and the omelette loses its spontaneity. Australian chef Bill Granger gave me a great tip to prevent last-minute overcooking: 'Always take the omelette out before you think it is cooked as it continues cooking off the heat.' But despite trying different cooking techniques, I still hadn't got the rhythm right and wondered how much I should beat the eggs, and should I add liquid?

Help from an expert

I called on Raymond Blanc, who told me, 'A great dish starts with the nobility of the produce and corn-fed hens' eggs are best.' So we tested eggs for freshness – break the egg on a plate and, if it's fresh, the white sits perkily and tightly round the yolk; if not, it looks watery and saggy.

Then he turned to my beating. 'Beat with a fork until the yolks and whites are broken, but not completely mixed – this gives more texture. As to adding liquid, 'I would for scrambled eggs as it softens them, but not to an omelette. Get everything ready before you start,' Raymond advised: 'an omelette won't wait.' As he tipped the eggs into the pan, it all became clearer. His technique – a combination of stirring and allowing the mixture to settle with a bit of shaking – created a smooth, firm outer egg-jacket, with a soft, gooey interior. The settling bit is important, if you only stir you'll end up with scrambled eggs. His omelette was 'blonde' (no colour) and expertly folded to look like a cigar. I would do the same shape, but make it a 'brunette' (tinged with brown). A brush with some butter gave a shiny, professional finish.

Fine-tuning the flavour

Before my final test, I bought eggs from Peter, my neighbour. They were so fresh, they were still warm. I consulted one more expert, Robert Carrier in France. 'I add two things that most people don't,' he revealed, 'an extra egg white, lightly beaten, and a sprinkling of Parmesan. You don't taste the Parmesan, it just makes an eggier omelette, and the white makes it fluffier.' I decided against the soufflé version, but loved the subtle savoury effect the Parmesan gave. So now I have my ultimate recipe. Do try it! I hope that it helps you to create yours.

1 Gently draw the mixture in from the sides so that it gathers in folds in the centre.

2 Stop stirring while there's some barely cooked egg left.

3 Fold the omelette over by a third and keep rolling it over so it tips onto a serving plate.

The recipe

Serves 1

Ready in under 5 mins

Easy
(once you get the hang of it)

What you need

- 3 eggs, as fresh as possible, preferably organic, room temperature
- 2 knobs of unsalted butter
- 1 tsp finely, freshly grated Parmesan

1. Get everything ready. Warm a 20cm/8in (measured across the top) non-stick frying pan on a medium heat. Crack the eggs into a bowl and beat them with a fork so they break up and mix, but not as completely as you would for scrambled egg. With the heat on medium-hot, drop one knob of butter into the pan. It should bubble and sizzle, but not brown. Season the eggs with the Parmesan and a little salt and pepper, and pour into the pan.
2. Let the eggs bubble slightly for a couple of seconds, then take a wooden fork or spatula and gently draw the mixture in from the sides of the pan a few times, so it gathers in folds in the centre. Leave for a few seconds, then stir again to lightly combine uncooked egg with cooked. Leave briefly again, and when partly cooked, stir a bit faster, stopping while there's some barely cooked egg left.
3. With the pan flat on the heat, shake it back and forth a few times to settle the mixture. It should slide easily in the pan and look soft and moist on top. A quick burst of heat will brown the underside.
4. Grip the handle underneath. Tilt the pan down away from you and let the omelette fall to the edge. Fold the side nearest to you over by a third with your fork, and keep it rolling over, so the omelette tips onto a plate – or fold it in half, if that's easier. For a neat finish, cover the omelette with a piece of kitchen paper and plump it up a bit with your fingers. Rub the other knob of butter over to glaze. Serve immediately.

Extra flavours
If you want to add something else, keep it subtle so as not to overpower the delicate taste of the eggs.

Cheese
Scatter on 3 rounded tablespoons finely grated Gruyère at the end of step 2.

Herb
Stir 2–3 chopped tarragon leaves, and 1 tablespoon each snipped chives and chopped chervil or parsley into the beaten eggs.

Scrambled Eggs

I hadn't realised how controversial scrambling a few eggs could be. Each recipe I looked at contradicted the previous one. While one told me to thoroughly beat the eggs, another suggested doing so lightly. I could melt butter in the pan before adding the eggs, or not. Milk or cream could either be beaten in with the eggs, stirred in after the eggs were cooked, or not added at all. I could cook the eggs fast or slow, in a saucepan, frying pan, double boiler or microwave. I was sure they all worked but which was best?

An Australian chef's secret

I contacted Australian chef Bill Granger, whose scrambled eggs (served in his brunch restaurants in Sydney) have been highly acclaimed around the world. His secret? 'Don't stir too much,' Bill said. 'Scrambled eggs is a bit of a misnomer, they should really be called "gently folded eggs". Where people go wrong,' he remarked, 'is that they cook the eggs too slowly.' Bill's fast method produces big soft folds of egg. I experimented with his technique of letting the egg and cream mixture sit briefly in-between stirrings, and although I ended up using less liquid than he suggested (Bill uses lots), I was impressed by the softness of the folds, almost omeletty. Using a small non-stick frying pan instead of a saucepan made this technique much easier too.

Now for something completely different

I thought I had cracked it, then doubt set in after reading a recipe that completely contrasted Bill's. It was by Matthew Fort in the *Guardian Weekend*. He wrote, 'Scrambled eggs are the apotheosis of slow food, because the slower they are scrambled, the better they will be.' Bill's took about one minute, Matthew's up to 40! This I had to try. It was tricky keeping the heat low enough, but I couldn't believe the result. The constant stirring made them incredibly creamy, even though no liquid was added, the velvety smooth texture reminding me of the slow French method done in a pan or doubler boiler. However, although I cut the stirring time down to 20 minutes, it still seemed too long for what is essentially a quick snack.

Perfecting the creaminess

I returned to Bill's method, spurred on by the creaminess of Matthew's. With both methods it was easy to overcook the eggs. What changed my thinking was a comment made by Margaret Costa in her *Four Seasons Cookery Book* (Grub Street), 'have the courage to take them off the heat before they have quite finished cooking.' This made it easier to prevent overcooking the eggs and keep them creamy. I scrambled eggs in the microwave (it was neither quicker nor better), then wanted to see whether adding liquid to the eggs before cooking, or stirring it in afterwards, made any difference to the creaminess. It didn't, it was just simpler when added before. Having discovered all sorts of ways to make scrambled eggs – I now know which one is my favourite.

The recipe

Serves 1 (easily doubled)

Ready in about 5 minutes

Easy

What you need

2 eggs, preferably organic, room temperature
2 tbsp single cream or full-fat milk
small knob of butter

1 Get your toast organised, so it's ready as soon as the eggs are. Beat the eggs with a fork until the yolks and whites are combined. Mix in the cream or milk. Season with pepper and salt just before you are ready to cook (if done too soon, the salt thins the eggs).
2 Heat a 20cm/8in non-stick heavy frying pan. Drop the butter in, it shouldn't burn, just sizzle and melt, then you know the temperature of the pan is right. Pour the egg mixture in over a medium heat. Let the eggs sit for 20 seconds, don't be tempted to stir, then very slowly, using a wooden spoon, fold the mixture from the edge of the pan into the centre a few times. If you forget the word 'scrambling' this may stop you over-mixing at this stage. Leave the mixture for another 10–15 seconds, then gently stir and fold again.
3 While the eggs still have some runniness (they should look as though they aren't quite cooked yet) take them off the heat. The heat from the pan will finish cooking them in the next few seconds as you gently stir. Tip them onto your hot buttered toast and serve as fast as you can.

Cooking tips

- This recipe makes scrambled eggs with big soft folds – if you prefer smaller curds, lower the heat slightly and stir the mixture more frequently as it cooks.
- For best results cook no more than four eggs at a time.

Macaroni Cheese

When I began my quest for the ultimate version of this essentially English Victorian supper dish, I decided it needed a 21st-century makeover. Motivated by my recollection of macaroni cheese as a potentially rather dry, heavy dish, often lacking in flavour, I scanned numerous recipes to find I was not alone in this belief. Many newer versions contained any one or more of the following that had been added to alter its make-up: pancetta, sundried tomatoes, mascarpone, ricotta, pesto, courgette, spinach, red pepper and even barbecued chicken. In need of a reality check, I called food writer Ruth Watson. She questioned why I wanted to update something that was so intrinsically good. 'The whole point is that it's macaroni cheese – English, not Italian. Leave well alone,' she advised.

Staying true

So, although tempted by an impressive looking souffléed version in Delia Smith's *How to Cook Book One* (BBC Books) and by another quick, no-sauce version (just cheese and cream mixed into pasta) – it was Gary Rhodes' strong belief in the classic, made with béchamel sauce, that made me determined to improve on that. I would address the type of cheese and pasta, the consistency of the sauce and find out how I could keep the dish moist, and inject flavour without indulging in unnecessary additions. As I went in search of macaroni, I could feel my resolve to remain true to the original slipping away. Pastas of all shapes and sizes vied for my attention. However, after various tests, none matched up to a good-quality macaroni. It proved to be the perfect size and shape, and allowed the sauce to hug it beautifully.

Choosing the cheese

Cheddar on its own in the sauce has often disappointed. Ruth suggested using a combination of cheeses. 'It needs to taste of cheese,' she remarked. 'That sounds odd, but often it doesn't. I use predominantly mature Cheddar, plus a little Parmesan and, as I like a bit of "goo", I use some Gruyère – for texture more than flavour.' Gary Rhodes suggested a mix, too. 'For a béchamel sauce, I use half Cheddar, half Gruyère. It gives more pull. Or two-thirds blue cheese and one-third Cheddar or Gruyère.' He explained that using just Cheddar can give an oily sauce as it can separate, especially if overcooked. I experimented with different cheese combinations and proportions, and was impressed by the unique characteristics a mixture brought to the sauce. The blend that won was made up of an aged Cheddar that provided the dominant flavour,

Gruyère that gave gooeyness to the texture, and Parmesan that offered extra bite. To balance the taste, I stirred in a touch of Dijon mustard (English was less mellow, wholegrain too bitty).

The correct consistency

I normally make a white sauce to a classic formula (25g/1oz each of butter and flour for the roux, followed by 300ml/½ pint of cold milk). The consistency is fine for pouring over fish or vegetables, but it quickly thickened when mixed with the pasta, causing the finished dish to be dry. Gary said he always adds a bit of extra milk to make the sauce thinner, as does Ruth. She also keeps adjusting the sauce: 'I simmer it gently for about 15 minutes for smoothness. If it needs more liquid, I adjust it at this point.' Simmering the sauce for longer than I usually do (but not as long as Ruth) made it both smoother and silkier, and adding extra milk later gave me more control over the consistency.

1 Add the warm milk in thirds and beat with a wooden spoon.

Changing the technique

Knowing how easy it is to end up with a lumpy sauce, I whipped up an all-in-one version, where all the ingredients go into the pan at once, to see if this method was more foolproof. It lacked depth, so I returned to the classic method and consulted *How to Cook Better* (Mitchell Beazley) by Michelin-starred chef Shaun Hill. He made two points which were to change my sauce-making technique forever. 'The traditional recipe calls for equal quantities of flour and butter, but the roux is easier to handle if the ratio of butter to flour is increased slightly,' he wrote. Shaun also added warm milk, not cold, in stages. This combined with the roux more easily and greatly reduced the risk of lumpiness.

2 Stir in the cheese and mustard, then add enough milk for a slack coating consistency.

Final adjustments

However, I knew things could still go wrong at the last stage, when the pasta and sauce came together. Too much or too little of either would ruin the dish. Ruth offered advice that helped me to work out the best amounts of each. 'When you put the macaroni into the sauce, it should be extremely well lubricated and thickly coated, but you don't want great pools of sauce lying around in the bottom of the pan.' Tipping the pasta into the pan of sauce enabled me to make more last-minute consistency adjustments. All I needed now was some contrasting colour and crunch. I remembered Ruth saying, 'I can't eat macaroni cheese without tomatoes.' Her idea of thick slices of tomatoes nestled in some cheesy crumbs offered protection to the macaroni as it was warmed through, as well as a colourful crisp topping. Not quite the makeover I had originally intended, but definitely one to be proud of.

3 Top the dish with the tomatoes before heating through in the oven.

The recipe

Serves 4 generously, with enough for seconds (easily halved)

Ready in about an hour

Fairly easy

What you need

175g/6oz mature Cheddar, such as Denhay
50g/2oz Gruyère
50g/2oz Parmesan
50g/2oz white bread, crusts cut off
3 medium tomatoes
280g/10oz good-quality macaroni
700ml/1¼ pints full-fat milk, plus a bit extra
50g/2oz butter
50g/2oz plain flour, minus 1 tsp
1 rounded tsp Dijon mustard

1 Making macaroni cheese is a bit of a juggling act, so it's easier if you prepare a few things ahead. Finely grate all the cheeses, keeping them separate. Tear the bread into pieces and whizz in a food processor to coarse crumbs. Mix 25g/1oz of the Cheddar and one-third of the Parmesan into the breadcrumbs. Toss the rest of the cheeses together and set aside. Thickly slice the tomatoes. Butter a dish, about 30 x 20 x 5.5cm/12 x 8 x 2¼in. Heat the oven to 190°C/fan 170°C/Gas 5.

2 Put a pan of water on to boil. Tip the macaroni into the boiling water, stir and bring it back to the boil. Simmer for 8 minutes, or cook according to pack instructions, stirring occasionally to stop it sticking. While this is cooking, start the sauce.

3 Warm the milk in a jug in the microwave (or in a pan). Melt the butter in a pan (big enough to take the macaroni as well), then stir in the flour. Cook for 1 minute, stirring, then take off the heat. Pour in one-third of the warm milk and beat well with a wooden spoon until smooth – it will be quite thick at this stage. Add another third – it may go a bit lumpy, but keep beating well and it will go smooth again. Pour in the final third of milk and keep beating until smooth.

4 When the macaroni is done, tip it into a colander and put it briefly under very hot running water to keep it separate. Drain. Put the pan of sauce back on the heat and cook, stirring, until thickened and smooth. Lower the heat and simmer for about 4 minutes until glossy, stirring every now and then. Remove from the heat and stir in the cheese and mustard, then beat in 5 tablespoons of milk, or enough to give a slack coating consistency. Taste and season (you shouldn't need much salt). If the macaroni is sticking at all, put it under the hot tap again, then stir to separate. Drain well, then gently mix it into the sauce and stir to coat completely. If necessary, adjust the consistency again with milk. There should be enough sauce to coat the macaroni thickly and liberally.

5 Tip the macaroni cheese into the buttered dish, scatter over the cheesy crumbs and lay the tomatoes casually over the top. Heat through in the oven for 12–15 minutes until beginning to bubble around the edges. Grill for 3–5 minutes to brown the crumbs. Let it all settle for 1–2 minutes, then serve while still piping hot.

Kedgeree

It took me a while to get to grips with the ultimate kedgeree. As Jennifer Brennan wrote in her cookbook of the British Raj, *Curries and Bugles* (Tuttle Publishing), 'The growth of the name is as lengthy as the transitions through which the venerable dish has gone'. Kedgeree began life in India as a lightly spiced staple of rice and lentils called *khichri*, before the British Raj turned it into a posh breakfast dish by replacing the lentils with fish, topping it with hard-boiled eggs and anglicising the name. Smoked fish eventually replaced the fried fresh fish used in India, peas were sneaked in and curry powder substituted whole spices.

Back to the beginning

I found endless possibilities regarding the spicing, rice and fish varieties, as well as versions that were either creamy, buttery, dry or soupy. So I sought advice from Namita Panjabi, director of the restaurant group Masala World, who grew up in Bombay. She explained how breakfast became a big institution for the British in India and that kedgeree would always have been one of the dishes laid out. Namita said, 'There is no right or wrong way to make a kedgeree – it depends on how light or luxurious you want it to be.' However, despite the fact that she told me that *khichri* means 'a big jamboree of all kinds of things', I didn't feel that gave me licence to throw in whatever I wanted. I liked the notion of kedgeree being luxurious, just as it had been in the days of the Raj, but didn't want to ignore its humble beginnings, so I asked for a few guidelines. 'It should be slightly moist and pale in colour. Don't add peas,' Namita advised, 'or powdered spices.' This was helpful, as I was in search of a more fragrant interpretation than my normal powdered spice version, with a lighter, moister texture. I had previously cooked everything separately, then gathered the ingredients together just before serving, but I felt that this approach never really unified the dish, or allowed the flavours to mingle and develop. If I could bring back some of the subtle spicing and traditional cooking techniques of the Indian *khichri* and combine it with the western additions of the British kedgeree without overcrowding the dish, this would become my ultimate version.

An unusual interpretation

I had been told about a unique version that has been on the menu at The Ivy since it opened in London in 1991. 'It's so popular I don't think we could take it off,' said head chef Alan Bird. A mix of smoked fish and sautéed oyster mushrooms is added to a delicately spiced cream sauce

that is poured over rice, topped with a poached egg and scattered with herbs. 'The curry cream sauce is our interpretation,' explained Alan. 'We strain the spices out so you get the flavour, but not the bits.' The cream kept everything moist, but I favoured something less saucy.

1 Stir the rice into the onions and spices.

Breaking old habits

Reluctant to give up on powdered spices, I cooked my usual version, made by poaching smoked haddock in milk very briefly (to keep it moist), frying leeks (trying to be different), curry powder, mustard powder and turmeric in butter, then stirring the spiced leeks into plain boiled rice with eggs and the flaked fish. The flavour was fine but lacked finesse. It was also dry, so I compensated by stirring in some of the fish poaching liquid (for flavour and moistness) and cream (for richness). I knew immediately that I wanted a more fragrant spiciness. I spoke to writer and broadcaster Roopa Gulati, who told me, 'I wouldn't use curry powder. It won't give you the elegance that comes from seeds.' Whole spices would give a more authentic Indian taste. This concurred with Namita's advice and I also wanted to try The Ivy's combination of smoked haddock and smoked salmon, for both colour and flavour contrast.

2 Simmer the rice with the flavourings until tender.

Tradition wins out

As I deliberated over how to create a more unified dish, I remembered Namita saying that kedgeree was a fusion of *khichri* and a *pilau*. This changed my whole thinking. Since the rice for a *pilau* is cooked with the spices in a measured amount of liquid, what if I cooked mine like that? It would inject more flavour into the rice from the start, and keep it moister. I could also cook the rice in the poaching milk for even more flavour. Namita and Roopa had mentioned butter as an important ingredient, so I dropped a knob of it onto the cooked rice. When I stirred it in with the big pieces of fish and lightly boiled eggs, everything was united in a moist butteriness with no need for cream or extra milk.

3 Gently stir in the fish flakes and coriander before adding the eggs at the end.

Balancing the spices

Since curry powder was out, I decided to use curry leaves. As I fried them with chopped onion and a few well-chosen whole spices, the aroma told me I was on the right track. Why had I ever been diverted by leeks when traditional onion is so magnificent in this dish? Nicely browned, it complemented the spices perfectly. A small amount of turmeric was giving the rice a hint of colour, but something was missing in the flavour. I tried boosting it by frying a little curry paste with the spices, but it detracted rather than assisted. Both Roopa and Namita had stressed the need for simplicity. 'It should be lightly spiced,' said Roopa, 'with some chilli, but not so that it catches the back of your throat.' I whipped out the bay leaf that had been flavouring the milk for the fish and dropped in a dried red chilli instead – finally, the discreet kick I was after.

Last-minute additions

Cooking the rice with whole spices was bringing me closer to my goal, but I still felt it needed an extra something. 'You could finish with lime and coriander,' said Namita. I loved the refreshing contrast they gave, but that wasn't it. 'My mum would put a tangle of crisp fried onions on top,' said Roopa. That was it. As I piled on my crisp onions, I knew I had found the crowning glory.

The recipe

Serves 4

Ready in 45 minutes

Easy

What you need

For the crisp onions

2 medium onions
2 tbsp vegetable oil

For the kedgeree

350g/12oz undyed smoked haddock
175g/6oz lightly smoked salmon fillet
1 dried red chilli
½ pint full-fat milk
3 tbsp vegetable oil
1 cinnamon stick
1 medium onion, chopped
about 14 fresh or freeze-dried curry leaves
4 cardamom pods, split
280g/10oz basmati rice
½ tsp turmeric
50g/2oz butter
2 eggs
handful of fresh coriander leaves and some lime wedges, to serve

1 For the crisp onions, first halve and very thinly slice the onions. Heat the oil in a frying pan, add the onions with a pinch of salt (which helps to stop them burning), then cook on a medium heat, stirring occasionally, until deep golden, about 20–25 minutes. When done, spread on kitchen paper and leave to crisp up. While the onions are frying, put both fish in a frying pan with the chilli. Pour the milk over, cover and simmer for 4 minutes. Take off the heat and let stand, covered, for 10 minutes to gently finish cooking the fish.

2 Meanwhile, heat the 3 tablespoons of oil in a deep frying or sauté pan (with a lid). Break the cinnamon into pieces and add to the oil with the onion, curry leaves and cardamom. Fry until the onion is soft and golden, about 7–8 minutes, stirring often. Lift the fish from the milk with a slotted spoon, discard the skin and any bones, cover to keep warm and set aside. Make the milk up to 600ml/1 pint with water. Rinse the rice in warm water in a colander, drain, then stir it into the onion. Keep stirring for 1 minute so the rice is coated. Pour in the milk mix and stir in the turmeric. Bring to a boil, then simmer for 10 minutes, covered, lowering the heat if it starts to stick on the bottom.

3 When the rice is tender, remove from the heat, drop the butter on top so it melts in, then lay the whole pieces of fish on the rice. Cover and leave for the flavours to mingle. Meanwhile, put the eggs in a pan, cover with cold water and bring to the boil, then boil for 6 minutes (for soft-boiled). Remove from the heat and plunge into cold water, cracking the shells against the side of the pan. Peel off the shells and quarter the eggs.

4 To serve, break the fish into big pieces, add the coriander and stir gently to mix without breaking up the fish, adding the eggs at the end. Season, scatter the crisp onions on top and serve with lime wedges.

3

ALL-TIME GREATEST SALADS

Greek Salad

Why is it I can eat bowlfuls of this salad while lazing over lunch in a Greek taverna but find it hard to sustain an interest in flavour and texture when eating it at home? The main reason, I realised, is that it is essentially a very simple salad made up of few ingredients, most of which are high on crunch, but not so strong on taste when out of their Mediterranean environment. Food writer Jennifer Joyce (author of *The Well-dressed Salad*, Pavilion) agreed. 'When you go to Greece and taste their version, it's perfect, but there you have sun-kissed ingredients. I love eating it all year round, but even if I have ripe tomatoes, it still needs something else. Although you want some kind of crunch, the texture requires balancing out. So many salad bars have demolished it and taken it away from how it should be, leaving it sitting in a pool of olive oil with nothing else interesting added to the dressing.' My aim would be to bring a little sunshine to the vegetables and dressing, without destroying the simplicity and crispness of this rustic salad.

More taste, less crunch

So what would turn my Greek salad around? I wouldn't digress from the main ingredients – tomatoes, peppers, cucumber, feta, onion, olives, oregano, olive oil – but I would find ways to bring greater variety to their texture and taste. Some recipes suggested tossing chopped Romaine lettuce leaves in – but this just added even more crispness without flavour. I liked the sweetness red onion offered over regular onion, but the taste was quite strong. I tried marinating it in lemon juice to tone it down, but found I preferred the raw intensity, so would just use less of it. The tomatoes had to be the reddest and ripest I could find for the sunshine factor – and vine-ripened won out hands-down. If I used the vegetables at room temperature rather than straight from the fridge, their flavour shone through. However, everything, apart from the feta, was still remorselessly crunchy. Wondering how to get a different texture in there, I remembered seeing a traditional recipe where the peppers were roasted rather than used raw. My preferred colour was red for sweetness, and roasting brought out this quality all the more, offering a contrastingly soft, juicy texture at the same time.

The dressing gets a makeover

I now needed to liven up the dressing. I had been mixing up a simple vinaigrette, but as yet it didn't have enough punchiness. Greek olive oil gave a fruity-herby taste, and lemon juice had the edge over wine vinegar – its sharpness complementing the sweetness I was now getting

from the peppers. Rather than falling back on garlic as a flavour booster, I looked to the herbs. Oregano is a classic and adding a pinch of dried certainly helped, but not enough. I chopped fresh oregano and mint together and more flavour came through when I scattered them through the salad rather than mixed them into the dressing. But herbs hadn't quite resolved things. I then noticed the juices oozing from the softened roasted peppers – so I quickly tipped the dressing in and let it all marinate. Everything flowed together, each flavouring the other. Now it was lively.

Getting it ready to serve

All I had to do now was amalgamate salad and dressing. I threw everything into a big salad bowl and gave it all an enthusiastic toss. As I glanced down, the feta had broken down too much and the salad looked muddled, not crisp and fresh enough – so I carefully piled it into individual bowls instead. Having discarded the idea of lettuce leaves, I felt that something green with a bit of bite to it on the bottom of each bowl would be a good idea. The complementary pepperiness of just a few sprigs of watercress worked perfectly. In Greece this salad is often served with wide slices of feta laid on top, which I tried to replicate. However, the feta I could buy easily wasn't wide enough for slicing and just fell apart. Instead I crumbled it over in big lumpy pieces. I began to tuck in, and by the time I got to the last mouthful realised it was so full of character, I could have eaten the whole bowlful all over again.

1 Grill the peppers, turning occasionally as each side blackens (using the stems as handles).

2 Lay the peppers in a shallow dish and pour the dressing over them.

3 Chop the cucumber and tomatoes, and slice the onion, then make up each salad individually.

The recipe

Serves 4

Ready in just under an hour (includes some marinating time)

Easy

What you need

2 red peppers
6 tbsp extra-virgin olive oil, preferably Greek
2 tbsp lemon juice
½ tsp freeze-dried oregano
½ cucumber
4 medium vine-ripened tomatoes
1 very small red onion
watercress sprigs, to serve
about 12 kalamata olives
200g/8oz Greek feta
2 sprigs fresh oregano
2 sprigs fresh mint

1 For the best flavour, take all the ingredients out of the fridge so that they can come to room temperature. Heat the grill. Put the whole peppers on a baking sheet and grill for about 25–30 minutes, turning occasionally as each side blackens (using the stems for handles), until the skins are blackened all over. Put the peppers in a bowl and cover with plastic film (or in a plastic bag and fold over the end) and leave to cool a bit (the steam created will make it easier to remove the skins).

2 While the peppers are grilling, whisk the olive oil and lemon juice together, stir in the dried oregano and season with a little salt and pepper. Peel the skins from the peppers, remove and discard the cores and seeds and cut the peppers into bite-sized pieces. Lay the peppers in a shallow dish and pour the dressing over them. Leave to marinate for a minimum of 15 minutes, or as long as you have time (this can be done overnight).

3 When you are ready to serve, chop the cucumber into chunks. Halve the tomatoes and cut out their cores, then chop into similar-sized pieces to the cucumber. Peel and halve the onion lengthways, then slice it very thinly.

4 Make up each salad individually by putting a few watercress sprigs in the bottom of four bowls. Scatter the cucumber, tomato and pepper chunks and olives over. Crumble the feta into biggish chunks and drop these on top. Pluck the leaves from the oregano and mint, roughly tear and scatter over. Spoon the dressing marinade from the peppers over each salad. Season with a fresh grinding of pepper.

Ingredients swap

Flat-leaf parsley can be used to replace the oregano, rocket leaves can replace the watercress.

Potato Salad

If I was to be influenced by the hundreds of recipes I found while researching this dish, it could have anything and everything mixed in, from crab and asparagus to apples, beetroot, caviar and pomegranates. Potato salad means different things to different people, depending on where you come from. Knowing how popular it is in North America, I contacted Lori Longbotham, cookbook author and a former Food Editor of *Gourmet Magazine* in New York. She confirmed my findings that classic potato salad can be American-, French- or German-style. 'In America, most are mayonnaise-based, many add celery, spring onions and lots of herbs,' she told me, 'while the old-fashioned kind has lots of chopped boiled eggs. In New York delis it's very loose and soupy, loads of mayonnaise, all white. They may salt the potatoes, but that's about it, the potato has no flavour, is waterlogged – and people eat it by the quart because they have grown up with it. It's a real New York thing. In California, now they will have a million different types. Occasionally people make a more European style.' According to *Joy of Cooking* (Simon & Schuster, USA), German-style features a hot bacon dressing, while the French, the authors write, 'like to bathe their potatoes in a simple vinaigrette. This needs to be done while the potatoes are still warm so they can absorb all the flavours of the dressing.'

To peel or not to peel?

I was spoilt for choice, so needed to narrow things down. I didn't want to make a meal out of this salad; it would be an accompaniment. For the potato, I've always had a soft spot for Jersey Royals, but knowing how short their season is, looked for another option. I knew a waxy variety would be best for salads, so boiled up some Nicola and Charlotte. I never bother peeling new potatoes, but wanted to see if it made a difference. It certainly did. When peeled, I was pleasantly surprised to see how the potatoes became more closely involved with the dressing. I then tried red-skinned varieties, having read many American recipes that favoured them. The yellow-fleshed Roseval was melt-in-the-mouth delicious, as was Pink Fir, and interestingly peeling spoilt rather than improved them.

Keeping it simple

For the dressing I tried tossing potatoes with mayonnaise, soured cream, crème fraîche, vinaigrette and varying combinations of all these, as well as adding different ingredients for crunch and flavour. The salad that stood out was the simplest – chunks of potatoes tossed while still warm in a chive and tarragon vinaigrette, allowing the flavour of the potatoes to emerge. Requiring nothing more than a scattering of crispy pieces of bacon for a contrasting crunch, I had ended up with a recipe influenced by the United States as well as Europe, but don't let this stop you from customizing your own version – the possibilities are still endless.

The recipe

Serves 4 (as a side salad)

Ready in 25–30 minutes

Easy

What you need

600g/1lb 5oz red-skinned salad potatoes, such as Roseval or Pink Fir
5 tbsp olive oil
½ tsp Dijon mustard
1½ tbsp white wine vinegar
2 rounded tbsp snipped fresh chives
1 tbsp finely chopped fresh tarragon
4 rashers unsmoked streaky bacon, snipped into small pieces with scissors

1. Cut the potatoes into big, even chunks. Drop them in a pan, cover with water, bring to the boil, and simmer for 10–15 minutes until just tender. (Test by pushing the tip of a sharp knife into the potato. If it goes in easily they are done.) Do not overcook or the potatoes will become waterlogged.
2. While the potatoes cook, make the dressing. Using a little wire whisk if you have one, or a fork, mix the olive oil and mustard, then whisk in the vinegar. Stir in the herbs and season to taste with salt and pepper. Dry fry the bacon in a non-stick pan over a medium-high heat until really crisp, stirring it around in the pan occasionally. Tip onto kitchen paper to drain.
3. Drain the potatoes in a colander so they are quite dry, and while still warm, tip them back into the warm pan and carefully toss with the dressing. Transfer to a salad bowl, scatter over the bacon, and finish with a grinding of pepper. Best eaten while still warm, or at room temperature.

Salade Niçoise

When I discovered Elizabeth David had written not just one version of salade Niçoise but four, in her *French Provincial Cooking* (Penguin Books), I knew this was going to be a controversial recipe. She describes it as 'a rough country salad, rather than a fussy chef's concoction,' suggesting that 'hard-boiled eggs, anchovy fillets, black olives and tomatoes with garlic in the dressing are pretty well constant,' then adds, 'It is up to you to choose the other ingredients,' offering as possibilities, 'tunny fish, cooked french beans, raw sliced red peppers, beetroot, potatoes, artichoke hearts.'

Lots of alternatives

After much research, I concluded there was not one definitive recipe, just as Elizabeth David had intimated. Sally Clarke of Clarke's in London agreed. 'The recipe is definitely open to interpretation. Niçoise suggests the coastal south of France, so it should have something fishy, fresh and crisp. A clutch of classic ingredients is a must. As long as it has tuna or anchovy or both, tomatoes and green beans, then possibly potatoes and possibly eggs, it can still be a type of salade Niçoise. Garlic is not necessary, you can make it taste fresh without.' Opinions were now divided about what the 'clutch of classic ingredients' should be, with eggs and garlic on Elizabeth David's essential list, but not on Sally Clarke's. Alex Mackay, cookery teacher and author of *Cooking in Provence* (Headline) offered a different view. Like Sally, he believes it evolved from people using whatever seasonal ingredients grew in their gardens in and around Nice, but he suggested that cookery writers from Nice insist on using only raw vegetables. 'Originally there would have been no tuna as that was expensive, so anchovies would be used instead. You want to have a mixture of ingredients with each forkful, so you need a balance, a mouthful of each, not a whole piece of tuna on top.' Alex described his ideal as a vibrant collection of crunchy fresh vegetables, such as cucumber, peppers, spring onions, artichokes, tomatoes and tender broad beans that don't need cooking, so the only thing to be cooked are the eggs. He would not add potatoes and definitely not lettuce: 'This is a salad that can sit and have all the juices converge. You can't do that if there is lettuce in.'

Clarifying the situation

I was now muddled, and Alex offered advice. 'It's about a combination of fresh ingredients served well, so the choice of them is very important, but you should go back to where it came from.' Sally had described this

salad as a summer combination with the notion of sunshine and sea – so I decided to concentrate on this in order to evoke its place of origin, at the same time being aware that the ingredients available to me would not be as sun-kissed as those harvested from Nice.

Making a few changes

For my first test I tossed cooked potatoes and green beans, wedges of hard-boiled eggs and tomatoes, some black olives, canned flaked tuna, a few anchovies and a basic oil and vinegar dressing. It was uninspiring and reminded me of the south of England rather than the south of France. Where was the sunshine, the warmth, the flavour? Each ingredient needed attention. Although I have always added potatoes to this salad, I agreed with Alex and out they went. I replaced them with chargrilled artichoke hearts, which proved much livelier and sunnier. I loved his idea of broad beans (they partner so well with anchovies) but couldn't get ones young and tender enough to eat raw. To keep cooking to a minimum I briefly cooked a few along with some green beans. The regular tomatoes I had used weren't providing enough flavour. 'Get whatever is ripest. Little plum tomatoes have an intense flavour in England,' Alex suggested, so I switched to these. I managed to hunt down the Niçoise olives and immediately more authentic flavours started happening. What about the fish? I didn't want to perch a piece of griddled tuna on top, so found quality, meaty fillets of tuna in oil that I wouldn't have to cook, plus plump marinated anchovies. Sally told me she sometimes uses quail eggs for a twist, but recalling how Elizabeth David had written about this as a 'rough country salad,' I wouldn't go fancy, just cook the eggs differently. 'You want the yolks to be still slightly soft,' Alex advised, so I cooked them for less time, and halved them to adorn the top of the salad. Everything was now in tune, except the dressing.

Livening things up

The straight oil and vinegar dressing I had been making was fine but uninteresting. Since lemons grow in the south of France, Alex advised using lemon juice instead of vinegar. When I tried this the dressing tasted too sour and harsh. No doubt the lemons I was using had not been recently blessed with sunshine, so a combination of white wine vinegar and lemon juice worked much better. However, it lacked excitement. 'It needs a kick of mustard,' Sally suggested. This helped, as did some fresh herbs, and although I had tried to avoid using garlic as it's used in so many other salads, I found that adding a little perked up the flavour. The salad was now ready to serve. Should I lay it out on a bed of lettuce as so

1 Trim the stalk ends of the green beans (not the tails).

2 Gradually pour the olive oil into the garlic, lemon juice, vinegar and mustard, whisking to make a dressing.

3 Stir in the herbs and season with salt and freshly ground pepper.

many restaurants do, or just toss the lot together? The lettuce wasn't necessary and I preferred Sally Clarke's suggestion of composing it in a haphazard way in a shallow bowl, so you can see all the ingredients clearly. So this is my interpretation, but to maintain the spirit of this salad, feel free to switch some of the ingredients around if you have ones with a sunnier disposition available.

The recipe

Serves 4

Ready in about 35 minutes

Easy

What you need

8oz/200g green beans
8oz/200g podded broad beans, fresh or thawed, if frozen
12 baby plum tomatoes, preferably on the vine
4 eggs
2 x 190g jars good-quality fillets of tuna in olive oil (such as yellow fin)
280g jar chargrilled artichokes in olive oil, drained (or buy 175g/6oz loose from the deli counter)
12 anchovy fillets in oil, drained
about 20 small black olives (not pitted), preferably Niçoise

For the dressing

1 small garlic clove
1 tbsp lemon juice
1 tbsp white wine vinegar
1 tsp Dijon mustard
6 tbsp extra-virgin olive oil, preferably a fruity one
2 tbsp each of chopped fresh oregano or marjoram and flat-leaf parsley

1 Have all your ingredients at room temperature so you get the best flavour. Trim the stalk ends of the green beans (not the tails) and steam for 3–4 minutes until bright green and still crisp. Cool immediately in a sieve under running cold water. Drain well. Cook the fresh (or frozen) broad beans in boiling water for 2–3 minutes, drain, cool slightly, then peel off the skins. Slice the tomatoes in half lengthways.

2 Make the dressing: crush the garlic, put in a bowl then whisk with the lemon juice, white wine vinegar and mustard, then gradually whisk in the olive oil. Stir in the herbs and season with salt and freshly ground pepper.

3 Put the eggs in a small pan, cover with water, bring to the boil, then boil for 6 minutes (for soft-boiled). Drain and cover with cold water, cracking the eggs against the side of the pan. Leave for about 4 minutes, then peel off the shells and halve the eggs.

4 Drain and break up the tuna into big chunky flakes. The salad is now ready to put together – preferably in wide, shallow bowls so you can see all the elements. Scatter in some of the green beans and a few broad beans, then divide the tomatoes, tuna, artichokes, anchovies, olives and the rest of the broad beans between the four bowls, keeping the arrangement casual and loose. Lay two egg halves on top of each salad and drizzle with the dressing.

Caesar Salad

If Italian chef Caesar Cardini had known how famous his salad would become the first time he spontaneously tossed it together at his restaurant in Tijuana, Mexico, I wonder whether he would have done it differently? Plenty of chefs have created more elaborate variations since, but I wasn't after a dolled-up version, preferring the simplicity of the original. This has become a mainstay restaurant salad, but Jennifer Joyce, author of *The Well-dressed Salad* (Pavilion), claims that they don't often get it right. 'Its usually too bland with not enough dressing which has too much oil. The ultimate should be a combination of tangy, salty and creamy. You need the balance of mustard, the crunch of the leaves and croûtons and the nuttiness of the Parmesan.'

Balancing out the flavours

Using a rustic French bread, I tackled the croûtons first by roughly ripping the bread then frying it in a mixture of oil and butter until crisp and golden. However, the pieces were too clumsy and greasy. They were far more stylish and easier to eat when cubed, tossed lightly in olive oil and baked. For the original salad, whole lightly coddled eggs had been ceremoniously broken over the dressed leaves. I decided against this, preferring the more popular interpretation of using just egg yolks as part of a creamy mayonnaise-style dressing. I played around with the number of garlic cloves and egg yolks, amount of mustard, oil and lemon, to get just the right balance of flavoursome creaminess, then thinned it with a drop of water so it would caress and coat rather than weigh down the leaves. Although there has long been a debate over whether anchovies should be included, I mashed a few and mixed them into the dressing. However, it lost its clarity and lightness. I loved the anchovy taste, so took them out of the dressing and instead tipped them in tiny pieces onto the leaves. This gave a perfect salty hit with each mouthful.

Some final adjustments

A crisp lettuce is paramount. I was using Cos for its shape as well as its crunch, and had no reason to change. A tip from Jennifer worked well too. 'Wash and dry the leaves, then leave in the fridge a bit. The water plumps them up, keeps them crisp.' According to *Joy of Cooking* (Simon & Schuster, USA), Caesar salad was 'originally made with whole leaves and eaten with the fingers'. Most recipes told me to tear the leaves, which I did to the bigger, outer ones for easy eating, but I kept as many as possible of the inner ones whole for the drama they provided. I didn't want to use my fingers to eat with, but did use them instinctively to toss the leaves – it seemed the gentlest way to prevent them from bruising. I leave you with the final decision – whether to grate or shave the Parmesan. My tasters were split, preferring shaved for the concentrated bursts of saltiness, grated for a more overall salty taste.

The recipe

Serves 6 as a starter
(4 as a main course)

Ready in 20 minutes

Easy

What you need
For the croûtons
140g/5oz rustic French bread
4 tbsp olive oil

For the salad
2 garlic cloves, chopped
1 tsp Dijon mustard
1 tsp Worcestershire sauce
1 tbsp lemon juice
2 egg yolks
125ml/4fl oz olive oil
2 heads Cos (or Romaine) lettuce, leaves separated, washed and dried
8 anchovy fillets, chopped into small pieces
50g/2oz piece of Parmesan, shaved or finely grated – the decision is yours

1 Heat the oven to 200°C/fan 180°C/Gas 6. Slice then cut the bread into rough cubes (about 1–2.5cm/½–1in) for the croûtons. Spread them in a single layer on a baking sheet, drizzle with the oil, then toss so all are coated. Bake for about 10 minutes until pale golden and crisp.
2 Meanwhile, mash the garlic to a fine paste with a pinch of salt (a pestle and mortar are perfect to use). Whisk in the mustard, Worcestershire sauce and lemon juice, then the egg yolks. Slowly drizzle in the oil, whisking all the time as you pour, until you get a dressing that is the consistency of double cream. Adjust the taste with lemon juice, salt and pepper – but remember the anchovy fillets and Parmesan will add saltiness too. If necessary, thin with a couple of teaspoons of cold water to get the consistency right so it will coat the leaves but not weigh them down.
3 Keep any small inner lettuce leaves whole, tear the larger outer leaves into 2 or 3 pieces and put them all into a large bowl. Pour the dressing over the leaves and carefully toss to coat them – using your hands is the gentlest way to do this (or use two forks). Either assemble in the bowl, or pile the leaves onto individual plates or bowls, giving each an equal share of whole and torn leaves. Scatter the anchovy fillets over, then the croûtons and Parmesan, and finish with a grinding of pepper.

Note: this recipe contains raw eggs.

Make it more substantial
To make even more of a main meal out of this salad, top with strips of pan-fried or roasted chicken, grilled salmon or pieces of crispy bacon.

Coronation Chicken

There's no doubting the enduring popularity of this lightly spiced salad, but I feel it has lost some of its dignity. It was considered most daring when created in the summer of 1953 by Rosemary Hume and Constance Spry, co-principals of the Constance Spry Cookery School, for an official celebratory lunch at the Coronation of HM Queen Elizabeth II. The cooked creamy sauce for the poached 'young spring chickens' was flavoured with curry powder, most unconventional at the time, and sweetened with apricot purée. I came across a popularised version by Marguerite Patten in her *Victory Cookbook* (Chancellor Press) which involved a simpler curry-flavoured mayonnaise dressing. But over the years this dish has been overused and abused. Could an update be due? I contacted Marguerite Patten for some background information.

A sign of the times

'It's a dish that can be very good or very bad,' Marguerite told me. 'I made it up for a party for neighbours on Coronation Day as we were the only ones with a TV. I'd heard about it and knew what it was vaguely, but not the details, so planned my own.' Like the original, hers involved poaching a chicken. Free-range chicken was not a term used then, she commented, as all chickens were organic. 'I cut the chicken into small bite-sized pieces so it was easy to eat, and drained and sliced canned apricots.' Some of the apricot syrup sweetened the mayonnaise for the dressing then curry and single cream (which had only just become available again) were stirred in. She used flaked almonds and a mixture of salad leaves for contrasting textures. 'These were the ingredients you could get without any trouble, though the choice of leaves was fairly conservative then.'

Giving it a culinary update

With the restrictions of the 1950s no longer in force, I asked Marguerite what she thought of a little tinkering. I wanted to freshen and lighten things up by mixing yogurt into the mayonnaise instead of cream, try mango instead of apricot, introduce fresh coriander and a different mix of salad leaves. 'The mayonnaise can be a bit overwhelming unless you do something with it,' Marguerite agreed. 'We didn't know yogurt in 1953, or mangoes,' but she approved of the makeover. Her parting advice (to maintain the original intent of the recipe) was to consider the delicate texture and colour of the dish. 'With the curry taste you only want a hint of it – it's not like eating a curry when you have more flavour. Nothing should overpower.' The chicken was definitely moister

Saving the stock
When the chicken stock has cooled completely, it can be frozen in handy-sized freezer containers for later use.

when poached, so I wouldn't alter that. I tried curry paste versus curry powder and was surprised to find I preferred the powder, and it gave a more rounded, delicate flavour to the dressing when cooked first in a spicy liquid. Chicory and Little Gem leaves gave the best crispness against the tenderness of the chicken and fruit, and the fresh taste of mango and coriander complemented the curry flavour without moving too far from the original. Though my changes may not be as daring as the original 1950s recipe, I hope they have helped to bring back some of this salad's dignity.

The recipe

Serves 6
(easily doubled for a bigger crowd)

Ready in about 2¼ hours (includes poaching the chicken), plus allow a few hours' cooling time

Easy

What you need

- 1.5kg/3lb 5oz organic chicken, the best you can afford
- 2 small onions
- 2 sprigs fresh tarragon
- 2 bay leaves
- 1 tbsp sunflower oil
- 4 tsp medium curry powder
- 2 tsp tomato purée
- 2 tbsp lemon juice
- 3 tbsp mango chutney
- 300ml/½ pint good-quality mayonnaise
- 150ml carton natural yogurt
- pinch of light muscovado sugar
- 20g packet fresh coriander
- 1 mango, peeled, stoned and sliced
- 2 Little Gem lettuce and 2 chicory

1. Sit the chicken in a large saucepan, then pour in enough water to just cover. Roughly chop one of the onions and drop it into the pan with the tarragon and bay leaves. Cover, bring to the boil, then lower the heat and let the water gently simmer for 1¼–1½ hours until the chicken is cooked. Test by lifting the chicken out of the water and sticking the point of a sharp knife into a fleshy part of it. If the juices run clear it is done. (If not, leave to simmer a little longer.) Return the chicken to the water, take the pan off the heat and leave the chicken to cool in the liquid for about 2½–3 hours. This keeps it moist. Lift the chicken from the stock and strain the stock, reserving 175ml/6fl oz. This can all be done a day ahead – then keep the chicken and stock in the fridge until ready to use.
2. Chop the other onion quite finely. Heat the oil in a frying pan and fry the onion for about 4–5 minutes until soft and pale golden. Stir in the curry powder and cook, stirring, for a minute. Stir in the reserved stock then the tomato purée and lemon juice. Simmer for 10 minutes. Remove from the heat, stir in the chutney, then strain into a bowl and leave to get cold.
3. Mix the mayonnaise and yogurt into the cold spiced liquid. Add the sugar, then taste and adjust the flavours if needed (it shouldn't be too sweet). Chill (or you can use straight away).
4. Strip the coriander leaves from their stems and roughly tear the leaves. When the chicken is cold, remove the skin and strip the meat into big chunky pieces, getting rid of any bones. Stir the chicken pieces into the curried sauce then gently stir in most of the mango slices and about half of the coriander. Separate the leaves from the Little Gem and chicory, then casually scatter them over one large platter (or two smaller ones) with most of the remaining coriander. Pile the chicken and mango mix on top, tuck in the rest of the mango slices to freshen up the look, and finish off with the last of the coriander.

4

EXCELLENT SOUPS AND BREADS

French Onion Soup

I never thought a bowl of soup could be so fascinating until I started researching this recipe. Since my last tasting of the French onion variety was not in a cosy Parisian café late at night, but in a Norfolk one at lunchtime, I decided I needed some authentic French advice on the genuine article. My first delvings were into Elizabeth David's *French Provincial Cooking* (Penguin Books). She wrote: 'The onion soup generally regarded as "French", with sodden bread, strings of cheese, and half-cooked onion floating about in it, seems to me a good deal overrated and rather indigestible.' This, then, was how it shouldn't be. A quick call to Anne Willan, who runs La Varenne cooking school in Burgundy, informed me of its origins: 'It is always served as a snack, traditionally in the middle of the night when you have been up late. The tradition started in the outdoor market of Les Halles in Paris, where the porters would stop and have a bowl of it.' Other sources claimed it could originally be a Lyonnais rather than a Parisian treat, and even more arguments emerged from my research as to how the soup should be prepared and served.

Red or yellow onions?

Chef Jean Christophe Novelli was adamant I use Saint André onions. Fine, except I wasn't sure where I could buy them. Anne Willan had an equally firm opinion. 'You need to use the strong yellow onions, none of this nonsense of using three onions of five different kinds.' I was also intrigued by another chef, who swore by red onions. My first attempt involved two batches, one with red onions, one with strong English ones. I cut them in semicircles rather than full circles, to make them easier to eat. The tears kept flowing as pounds of onions later I chose my favourite variety – the large yellow Spanish onion. Red were a little too sweet and gave the soup a rather dark, gloomy look. I tried the trick of stirring in a splash of balsamic vinegar to counteract this. It brought its appearance to life, but I favoured the cleaner, richer look the yellow onions gave. In all other aspects – flavour, cooking and availability – they were top of my list, too.

Homemade stock?

I went the purist route first of all, buying beef and chicken bones and simmering and reducing my stock for hours. Of course the taste was good, but it took too long. Beef stock rather than chicken was giving me the deep savoury taste and colour I was after, so I experimented with canned consommé. A combination of consommé with some white

wine, and the chef's trick of crumbling half a stock cube in at the end to intensify the flavour, became my favoured cheat's stock, ready in minutes rather than hours.

Cook it long and slow

It soon became clear that the cooking of the onions is where both the colour and flavour originates. Anne Willan's advice was ringing in my ears: 'They must be very well browned in butter. It might take 45 minutes and until they are almost burnt is fine.' Timidity is out of the question. You start off with a full pot and end up with an amazingly thin layer of concentrated flavour. To get the balance of meltingly soft onions combined with that lovely crisp caramelisation, it worked best to stir them frequently for the first 20 minutes, then let them cook undisturbed, apart from the occasional peep. I learnt this after one test when I thought they were sticking, so gave them a good stir towards the end of cooking. The resulting soup wasn't nearly as good. Caramelisation was better using a regular pan rather than non-stick. Adding the stock gradually enabled me to deglaze the pan easily, giving more richness to the colour. And when I forgot the bay leaf on one test, the difference was marginal. I also found that thickening with a little flour took away from the clarity of the broth and was not necessary. Although delicious, the soup still needed an extra something. I poured in a couple of spoonfuls of cognac and served it straight away. The raw alcohol taste spoilt the soup, but a little cooking really lifted it.

Finishing touches

London-based French food writer Marie-Pierre Moine told me she serves the soup with 'plenty of thick-cut, garlic-rubbed crisp toast on top, with lashings of grated Gruyère'. I tried the bread both toasted and

1 Peel and cut the onions through the root end, then slice with the flat-side down.

2 Make sure you slice the onions thinly before cooking very slowly.

3 As the onions reduce right down, check occassionally to make sure they aren't burning.

route, but took up his suggestion of using leeks instead of onion. Stock and cream were now providing the best consistency (milk tended to curdle), and having seen chilli mentioned in some recipes, a hint of it was all the extra flavouring I needed. Jasper gave me a parting tip, 'give it plenty of time to cure' (this means resting it for a deeper flavour and richer texture). As I looked at my bowlful I was convinced curing worked but am afraid I couldn't wait to try. I may have thought I already had a good chowder recipe but now I knew I had a *really* good one.

The recipe

Serves 4 as a light lunch or supper (easily halved)

Ready in 40–45 minutes, plus 1 hour's 'curing' time if you want

Easy

What you need

200g packet lardons
1 large knob of butter
2 leeks (about 350g/12oz), thinly sliced
1 tbsp fresh thyme leaves
small pinch of crushed dried chillies
2 bay leaves
650g/1lb 7oz potatoes, Desirée are good, peeled and sliced thickly (about 5mm/¼in thick)
700ml/1¼ pints fish or chicken stock (from a good-quality cube or powder is fine)
450g/1lb skinless haddock (the fish should be a firm and lean variety)
150ml carton single cream
roughly chopped fresh parsley for scattering

1 Heat a wide deep sauté pan. Tip in the lardons and fry until they have released their fat and have started to go crisp. Remove them with a slotted spoon and drain on kitchen paper, putting to one side for later. Drop the knob of butter into the pan and, as it sizzles, add the leeks, thyme, chillies and bay leaves and stir-fry for 2–3 minutes until starting to soften, but still bright green.

2 Tip in the potatoes, fry for a couple of minutes, stirring occasionally, then pour in the stock (it should just cover them). Boil over a high heat for 10 minutes, uncovered, until they are almost cooked through. (No need to stir as the potatoes may break up.) As they boil, their starch will be released and start to thicken the liquid.

3 Lay the whole fillets of fish on top of the potatoes so they are immersed as much as possible in the stock. Cover and simmer for 4 minutes. Remove from the heat, and let sit, still covered, for 5 minutes so the fish can finish cooking gently. Pour in the cream and shake the pan (rather than stir) so it mixes in, as you don't want to break up the potatoes and fish. Season with pepper – you may not need salt, depending on the stock you have used. The chowder can now rest for an hour or overnight in the fridge, which gives the flavours a chance to develop more. This is called 'curing'.

4 To serve, scatter the lardons over. Warm the chowder gently, being careful not to let it boil. Lift the fish and potatoes out with a slotted spoon, letting the fish break into very big chunks as you do so. Pile them both in the centre of wide shallow bowls or plates. Spoon the liquid around and scatter with the chopped parsley.

Watercress Soup

When I lived in Canada there was a cool stream running alongside the lane I lived on, and in the spring the banks became alive with watercress. I wish I could say I used to wander down and collect big bunches of it to make watercress soup on a regular basis – but sadly I never did. However, that image stayed with me while working on this recipe, to remind me of the fresh taste and lively colour I was after. During initial research I was lured by a very simple version using just watercress, onion and stock. So for my first test I gently cooked the onion in oil, tipped in some stock, then the watercress, and after a little simmering, everything was buzzed in the blender. Ten minutes later I was sipping on a bowlful but both the colour and flavour lacked depth, and with only watercress for thickening, the soup separated. I wanted simplicity, but not at the cost of taste and texture.

Other possibilities

After further research I discovered two more possible paths I could take: I could add bulk and stability with potato (but would I lose the lightness I was after?) or I could follow the French way of making a *velouté* – a saucy, creamy soup made so by thickening and enriching with flour, butter and milk, or egg yolk and cream. The latter would be more involved and I feared it would it be too thick and too rich. I sought the advice of French chef and restaurateur Regis Crepy at The Great House in Suffolk. 'When you make watercress soup as a *velouté*,' he told me, 'it is richer and heavier, and the taste of watercress may not be so strong.' I made up a batch and agreed. The soup was exceptionally silky but the creaminess was subduing the lively colour and flavour I was after.

Sorting out the texture

So I returned to simplicity, and would try thickening with potato rather than a roux. I found the proportion of potato to watercress used in recipes varied hugely from one potato to 675g/1lb 8oz watercress to 450g/1lb potato to a mere 50g/2oz of watercress. Regis Crepy had told me I should be serious about the watercress and add lots, so I sensed I needed just enough potato to bring the soup together without bulking it out. I spoke with Joyce Molyneux who confirmed this. She had frequently made watercress soup at the Carved Angel in Dartmouth which she once owned. Her version didn't involve a sauce and the beauty of it, she remarked, was its freshness. 'It doesn't have the sludgy look watercress soup sometimes has. Often not enough watercress is added.' She would add potato, 'but not too much,' she said, 'just a bit to

bind'. Her suggestion of 100g/4oz potato to 1 litre/1¾ pints of stock seemed to be hardly worthwhile, but it worked perfectly, and the density of the saucy version was gone.

Some great tips

My favourite tip of Joyce's though was to use the watercress stems (for flavour) as well as the leaves, something she had picked up from food writer Margaret Costa and something other recipes tell you to throw away. It reminded me of Thai cooks who prize coriander stems for the same reason, so it made complete sense. Separating the leaves from the stems proved time-consuming, but it was time well spent. As I stirred the chopped stems into the onions while they fried, the unique watercress scent drifted up to me immediately. Joyce's method was bringing me closer to my ultimate, combined with an idea I had read about in *Chez Panisse Vegetables* (Harper Collins), by American author Alice Waters. Instead of simmering the watercress in the soup (I was finding that even after a few minutes the vibrancy disappeared), she suggested adding it off the heat then letting the soup sit for 5 minutes. As the delicate leaves gently wilted in the soup's warmth rather than being stunned by direct heat, their colour and flavour remained intact.

Getting rid of the bitterness

I was still detecting some bitterness, a common complaint with this soup that I was eager to eliminate. I discovered a solution for this quite unexpectedly. Recalling a recipe of Gary Rhodes, where he added peas to watercress soup, I threw in a handful. I imagined they would bump up the colour, but I hadn't bargained for the edge of sweetness they contributed, and all the bitterness immediately disappeared. It only needed a small amount, as too many peas overpowered the flavour. I was

Serving tips

- Goes really well with the Irish soda bread on page 90.
- To reheat the soup, do so gently and briefly, or you will lose the colour.

1 Give the watercress a quick rinse if it needs it, then pluck the leaves from the stems.

2 Heat the butter in a medium pan, add the onion and the chopped watercress stems.

3 Remove from the heat and add the watercress leaves into the liquid.

also now using butter instead of oil for frying the onion, which gave a subtle richness, and a mild-flavoured stock rather than milk or cream was keeping everything light and bright. To complement the subtlety of the peas, I threw in a little chopped mint at the end, the cream became no more than a dashing flourish on each serving and the taste was now just how I wanted it.

Simplicity wins

Before offering my final version, there was one more thing to try. I wanted to know whether passing the soup through a mouli or sieve would improve the texture. But when sieved, half the goodness was left behind, and a thorough puréeing in the blender was much easier and all that was required. Simplicity had won out again for my very colourful, lively-tasting soup.

The recipe

Serves 4

Ready in about 40 minutes

Easy

What you need:

2 bunches watercress or 2 x 100g bags
1 medium onion
25g/1oz butter
1 small potato, such as Maris Piper or King Edward (100g/4oz), cut into small cubes
1 litre/1¾ pints good-quality vegetable stock
50g/2oz frozen peas
8 fresh mint leaves, very finely chopped
single cream for drizzling

Can be frozen

1 Give the watercress a quick rinse if it needs it, then pluck the leaves from the stems. Keep them both separate. Get rid of half the stems including any particularly thick ones and roughly chop the rest (the more tender ones). Chop the onion.
2 Heat the butter in a medium pan, add the onion and the chopped watercress stems and fry gently for 4–5 minutes, until the onions are soft and translucent, not brown. Add the potato and stir for a minute, then pour in the stock. Bring it up to the boil then simmer for 20 minutes, uncovered. Tip in the peas and simmer for 3 minutes.
3 Remove from the heat and stir the watercress leaves into the liquid. Leave for 5 minutes. This will allow the watercress to wilt without losing its colour, and for the soup to cool slightly before being blended.
4 Purée in a blender or food processor until smooth. Pour the soup back into the pan, stir in the mint and warm it through without letting it come to the boil or you will lose the colour. Taste and season if necessary. Serve with a creative drizzle of cream.

Carrot and Coriander Soup

It's a great combination, but I never did discover when coriander became an integral part of carrot soup. Looking at recipes by food writers such as Elizabeth David and Jane Grigson, coriander was nowhere in sight. Instead parsley and chervil were the flavourings of the day. Since carrot and coriander has become such a popular supermarket soup, I bought a tub just to check out the competition. There was much to improve on – it had little coriander flavour and the texture was starchy. For my first attempts I kept the ingredients simple, plenty of carrots, a little onion, a touch of potato for thickening (flour created the starchiness), butter, stock and fresh coriander, thinking that if I added enough carrot with coriander as a back-up, that would be all the flavour needed. There was nothing wrong but the soups could have been much better. I decided that fresh coriander on its own wasn't enough to add interest to the carrot.

Bumping up the flavour

In search of a more vibrant taste, I checked out contemporary writers such as Alice Waters and Sally Clarke. Their recipes included spices as well as herbs, either fresh chillies, or chillies combined with coriander and cumin seeds along with a generous bunch of fresh coriander. Surely these would add a welcome intensity? Also, I would make use of the coriander stalks as well as the leaves, since they have flavour pumping through them. I then recalled a spiced pumpkin soup of Nigel Slater's I had once tried, very simple, but coriander and cumin seeds were toasted until fragrant and nutty, and the whole soup was whizzed with a little dried chilli. The flavour was so alive and I wanted to bring something of that to this soup. Toasting then grinding the dry spices brought out far more flavour than when they were added raw but I added too many the first time and they overpowered the carrot, so I adjusted the amount and the taste was just what I had hoped for – a fresh and light, sweet carrot base, followed by a fragrant hit of spices.

Discovering a new topping

Wondering whether cream would add anything, I tipped a carton in at the end, but it just gave a richness that the soup didn't need, a paler colour, and clashed with the fresh spiciness. A small squiggle on the top of each bowlful looked decorative, but I was after something new, something with more flavour. Then food writer Val Barrett described a carrot soup she had once eaten that was topped with a coriander oil. It sounded like the perfect solution. I whizzed oil and fresh coriander together and drizzled it over the cream. Immediately there was no doubting the flavour of this soup, and spooning through the colourful drizzle of oil just intensified the whole experience.

The recipe

Serves 4

Ready in
about 40–50 minutes

Easy

What you need
25g/1oz butter
1 tbsp sunflower or vegetable oil
1 onion, chopped
2 plump garlic cloves, roughly chopped
40g bunch coriander
500g/1lb 2oz carrots, peeled and sliced
1 small potato (100g/4oz), peeled and diced
1½ tsp coriander seeds
½ tsp cumin seeds
¼ tsp crushed dried chillies
850ml/1½ pints good-quality vegetable stock
3 tbsp extra-virgin olive oil
single cream, to serve

Can be frozen

1 Heat the butter and oil in a large saucepan. Tip in the onion and garlic and fry for 5–6 minutes until soft and translucent but not browned, stirring occasionally. Pluck the coriander leaves from their stems, then chop all the stems and stir them into the pan with the carrots and potato. Cook over a low heat for 10 minutes, stirring occasionally.

2 Meanwhile, toast the coriander and cumin seeds in a dry pan over a medium heat for a minute or two until they start to smell fragrant. You don't want them to burn. Grind them to a fine powder using a pestle and mortar. Stir these into the carrot mixture with the chillies. Fry for a minute, then pour in the stock. Bring to the boil, lower the heat and simmer, covered, for 20–25 minutes until the carrots are soft.

3 While the soup is simmering, finely chop half the coriander leaves and set aside to stir into the soup later. Chop the rest of the leaves to make some coriander oil. Put them into a bowl and pour in the olive oil. Whizz with a stick blender to make a thin paste (this is your coriander oil), or if you don't have a stick blender or small processor, very finely chop the coriander and stir in the olive oil.

4 Let the soup cool for a few minutes, then pour it into a blender and whizz until smooth. Taste and adjust the seasoning with salt and pepper, though depending on the stock you've used, you may not need any. Pour the soup back into the pan. Stir in the reserved coriander leaves and gently reheat. Serve with a squiggle of cream topped with a drizzle of the coriander oil.

Irish Soda Bread

A bit of gentle handling – that's all soda bread asks for. The more experts I spoke to the more I realised that this is what is required, more than anything else, for an authentic light-textured, shapely loaf. It's not like making a traditional yeast bread. 'Think scones,' said chef Shaun Hill, who was born in Northern Ireland. 'The dough should be wettish,' advised Darina Allen who runs the Ballymaloe Cookery School in Ireland, 'and absolutely no kneading.'

Understanding the ingredients

I was already getting a feel for the raw dough, seeing that it should be soft, and definitely wouldn't respond well to over-handling, but what about the ingredients? There aren't many, and since Darina Allen had told me how different the flour is in Ireland, would my soda bread be authentic? I spoke to Stephen Odlum from the Irish miller Odlums Flour, who told me, 'Irish flour is made from soft Irish wheat, which makes a softer flour with a lower protein.' Odlums' baking technologist, Charles Burton, suggested I use a good-quality medium-strength plain flour. (Darina warned against a strong bread flour as the gluten level would be too high.) I could use all white or all wholemeal flour, but Charles recommended a combination. 'It gives you more lightness in texture and structure, rather than all wholemeal which makes the bread firmer, heavier.' He continued, 'adding bicarbonate of soda is traditional, it generates gas. Another vital ingredient is buttermilk. It gives a unique flavour and, when combined with the bicarbonate of soda, leaves a tingle on the tongue. The amount of buttermilk is very important, if you don't use enough you won't get the right shape or texture.'

Working with the dough

I was now ready to start mixing, so measured, stirred and shaped my first loaf. As I did so, it brought up more questions about the handling of it. What was the best way to mix the dough – with hands or a knife? I knew I should hardly be handling it at all but then how could I get it to come together? As for the dough, how wet is 'wettish'? This first attempt was too soggy – the bread just flattened as it baked. Trying to be practical I had used the whole cartons of buttermilk, but it was too much. I then tried it with less, but even before the bread went in the oven I could tell it was too dry and heavy. I settled on an amount in between. Darina then offered some handling advice. 'Get a big bowl,' she said. 'In the cookery school we fight over big washing-up bowls for this. You can make it in a smaller bowl, but you are constricted.

It's important to add the buttermilk all in one go, otherwise you'll get a heavier loaf as the liquid doesn't go in so well. Then stir in a circular movement, with your hand made like a claw so it is stiff and outstretched.' Feeling more confident, I tried again. Darina had told me some of the traditions that surround soda bread, and I could tell these would provide authenticity. 'Before baking the bread, cut a deep cross in it. This is called "blessing the bread". Then prick it in the centre of the four sections to let the fairies out. Also, always break soda bread in the centre to bring you good luck.'

In and out of the oven

The bread was ready to bake. After starting it at a high temperature then lowering it, then baking another loaf extremely high, a constant 200°C/fan 180°C/Gas 6 was the kindest, but I still felt the bread could be lighter and a bit tastier. Up until now I hadn't added any fat, but when Shaun Hill mentioned he mixed in some butter for texture and taste, I thought this might help. Charles Burton agreed: 'It is important to get flavour into the product, so you need to play around. Some traditionalists say you don't need fat, but I think you get a better texture and structure with a bit of it.' So I did play around, first adding oil (but this closed up the texture) then butter (much tastier, more open).

1 Stop handling it as soon as you have a soft sticky dough.

2 The dough shouldn't be kneaded, just gently tucked and eased into a round shape. The less it is handled the better.

3 Cut a deep cross on the surface of the dough with a sharp knife. This is called 'blessing the bread'.

Help from the fairies

I wasn't quite there yet as opinions were now divided about the crust. Though some tasters liked the crustiness of it, I favoured something softer. This was easily resolved, according to Darina. 'If you don't like it hard, wrap the bread in a tea-towel to soften the crust after baking.' I'm not sure whether it was luck, or the fairies, perhaps both, but as I carefully broke into my final test, I could tell it was the lightest, tastiest, most shapely soda bread I had ever made.

The recipe

Makes 1 loaf

Ready in 40–45 minutes

Easy, as long as it's treated gently

What you need

225g/8oz plain flour, preferably organic
225g/8oz plain wholemeal flour, preferably organic
2 tsp bicarbonate of soda
1 tsp salt
25g/1oz butter, room temperature
500ml/18fl oz buttermilk

Can be frozen

For a crisp crust
This recipe gives a loaf with a soft crust. For a crisp top, leave the loaf unwrapped as it cools.

1 Heat the oven to 200°C/fan 180°C/Gas 6. Butter and flour a large baking sheet. Mix both the flours with the bicarbonate of soda and salt in the biggest bowl you have – the bigger the better to give yourself room for the mixing. Cut the butter into pieces and rub it into the flour mixture so it is evenly mixed in.

2 Give the buttermilk a good stir. Create a big dip in the flour mixture and pour in the buttermilk all at once. You can now mix everything with your hands, or if you find it easier, start with a round-bladed knife to work in the liquid, then switch to your hands to finish off. Start in the middle of the bowl and work towards the outside in a circular movement – the mixing should only take a few seconds. (Darina Allen's tip.) You want to blend rather than mix, and if you do this for too long the dough will lose its lightness – so stop handling it as soon as you have a soft, sticky dough.

3 Tip the dough onto a lightly floured work surface. With floured hands, gently shape the dough into a round. It shouldn't be kneaded, just gently tucked and eased into a round shape. The less it is handled the better. Lift it onto the baking sheet. Pat it, again gently, into a round about 3cm/1¼in thick and 20cm/8in across, that is very slightly rounded at the top. Cut a deep cross on the surface of the dough with a sharp knife. Prick in the centre of each cut and sprinkle the loaf with a little flour.

4 Bake for 30 minutes until golden on top. Check the underneath before removing – it should be golden and sound a bit hollow when tapped. Transfer to a wire rack, and for a soft top, lightly wrap it with a clean tea towel as the loaf cools. To serve, break the bread in the centre (for luck), then into quarters and cut into thickish slices. Best eaten fresh, while still just a bit warm, but if well wrapped will keep for a couple of days.

White Loaf

If you think making bread is not for you – it's too tricky and there's too much kneading – this recipe could change your mind. Traditional techniques have been challenged, making it much easier to achieve a great-tasting white loaf. I can't claim the recipe as my own – the majority is all down to baker Dan Lepard.

A more relaxed approach

There's nothing different about the ingredients, it's the method that's surprising. 'Baking bread used to be about the labour of baking, the effort of kneading, rather than the flavour and the chemistry of the flour and water. My approach is to slow the process down, not put as much energy into the dough. You can achieve a good loaf with a softer dough and less kneading,' said Dan. 'The geometry of an English loaf tin is important – it gives the loaf a certain majesty. All it needs to look good is a curvy top and straight sides. The crumb should be fluffy with some substance, but not too tight, and you want the sense that hands have made it rather than a machine.'

Some chemical wizardry

As we began testing (mixing with our hands) we compared milk versus water as the liquid. Finding that milk slightly altered the taste, we chose water. Though Dan prefers to use fresh yeast, I was eager to go for the convenience of dried. 'If you get it activated first by letting it froth up,' said Dan, 'dried will have more life, and will then work the same as fresh.' The liquid went in (we added more and it was cooler than I would normally use) and the dough was so sticky I wondered how we would handle it. Dan reassured me, 'after working with sticky Italian doughs, I tried putting oil on the work surface instead of flour. It makes the dough easier to handle, stops it from drying out and keeps it light.' I now had to resist kneading the dough to develop the gluten in the flour, believing this was the best way to a well-risen loaf. Dan explained why he believed it wasn't. 'Gluten is developed as soon as the water goes into the flour, through hydration, over a period of time, not through kneading.' So instead of rocking back and forth for 10 minutes in an energetic frenzy, I calmly folded and kneaded the dough a dozen times only, then let the flour and water do their chemical wizardry on their own, repeating the process at intermittent intervals. Back in my own kitchen I continued tweaking. Instead of frothing up the dried yeast, I stirred it straight into the flour. This worked just as well and simplified the recipe even more. I also added some butter which lightened the

Make it wholemeal
Instead of using all white flour, use 250g/9oz strong white bread flour and 250g/9oz strong wholemeal bread flour.

texture and gave extra flavour. You are unlikely to get rid of any aggressions making this, but you will create a loaf full of character and flavour without too much effort.

The recipe

Makes 1 loaf

Ready in about 3½ hours (but most of this time is letting the dough stretch and rise on its own)

Fairly easy

What you need

- 500g/1lb 2oz strong white bread flour
- 1 tsp fast-action (also called easy-blend) dried yeast
- ½ tsp caster sugar
- 1½ tsp salt, preferably fine sea salt
- 25g/1oz butter, room temperature, cut into small pieces
- sunflower, vegetable or olive oil

Can be frozen

1. Tip the flour into a large bowl. Mix in the yeast, sugar and salt. Rub the butter into the flour. Make a dip in the centre of the flour and stir in 375ml/13fl oz water on the cold side of tepid. Mix with a knife or your hand then quickly knead together, squeezing with your hand to get the flour and liquid combined. The mixture will feel very sticky. Scrape off any dough that is left sticking to your hands. Leave the rough-looking dough in the bowl, cover with a clean tea towel and let stand for 15 minutes.
2. It will now feel slightly puffy. Spread about a teaspoon of oil on the work surface and rub a little on your hands too. Tip the dough onto the work surface and turn and fold to knead 12 times only. This is all the kneading that is required at this stage. The dough will feel smooth with little bubbles forming on the surface. Return it to the bowl rounded-side up. Cover and leave for 10 minutes. Repeat this twice more at 10-minute intervals. Now, knead the dough once more for 12 times only, then put the dough back in the bowl, rounded-side up, and leave, covered, for 30 minutes. Butter (or oil) and flour a 2lb loaf tin, preferably straight-sided.
3. Knead the dough 3–4 times just to knock out some of the bigger air bubbles, but no more as you want to keep the dough light. Cut the dough into 2 even pieces with a sharp knife. Sprinkle a little flour on the work surface and on your hands (not too much or you will dry out the dough). To shape each piece of dough into a taut ball, hold your left hand out as though you are going to shake hands. Holding it firm and upright, rest the thin edge of your palm on the work surface. Put one piece of the dough next to your hand and push it along the surface, letting the dough roll over very slightly until you can see it bulging, but not too much. Give a quarter turn and repeat. Do this 3 more times. Repeat with the other half of dough. Carefully place each piece of dough into the tin, side by side. Cover with a tea towel and leave to rise for 1–1½ hours until it is about 2.5cm/1in above the top of the tin (it may need longer if it's a cold day).
4. Heat the oven to 200°C/fan 180°C/Gas 6. When ready to bake, sieve a little flour over the loaf, then bake for 35–40 minutes until it is pulling away slightly from the sides of the tin, and the top, sides and base are golden. Loosen the sides with a round-bladed knife and remove the loaf from the tin straight away, or it will sweat in the tin. It should sound slightly hollow when you tap it underneath. Leave on a wire rack to cool.

Pizza

As with many culinary inventions, pizza was discovered quite by accident. The story of its creation varies with every storyteller. This is food writer Ursula Ferrigno's version: 'It began with people who were poor and under pressure to feed the family. Someone threw a crust of bread into the oven, a tomato followed and pizza was born.' From these humble beginnings, the thin-crusted, unpretentiously topped pizza has gone through many changes, especially in the United States. Here the crust got fatter and the toppings more extravagant. Authenticity was lost and, as Keith Floyd warned in *Floyd on Italy* (Michael Joseph): 'Toppings are what you fancy, but please don't turn it into a culinary dustbin.' Wanting to celebrate the original pizza's simplicity, I decided to work on the classic Margherita, named after Queen Margherita, but even this was complicated. As Anna Venturi, teacher and food writer, explained: 'There are two different types of pizza. The sort made in a pizzeria in a wood-burning oven with a thin, crisp crust, or one made in a domestic oven – the outcome is different.' In order to preserve the classic pizza's authenticity, Anna told me, professional pizza makers must stick to strict guidelines introduced by the Italian government. To be an accredited *pizzaiola* – pizza maker – you have to follow the rules, such as to cook the pizza in a wood-burning oven, give the dough a slow rise of several hours, then stretch it by tossing it in the air with all the skill of a juggler (the use of a rolling pin is not allowed). 'The challenge for home cooks,' said Ursula, 'is to create the classic pizza without a wood-burning oven.'

Going the traditional route

I began by running through some traditional dough-making techniques with Ursula. 'Use a strong white flour and olive oil,' she advised, 'not extra-virgin as it is too heavy and would ruin the dough. Add enough water so you have a soft dough. If too dry, it will be heavy.' We began kneading. 'Get into a rhythm, with one foot in front of the other to get your body involved. Watch the amount of flour on the work surface; too much and the dough will be dry. It should feel tacky.' We compared a slow-rise dough against a fast-rise one. The slow had all the desired characteristics, good texture, easy to work with and a well-developed flavour. The fast version was fine, but it was still too lively, so was more spongy and kept bouncing back while being rolled out. The winner wasn't in doubt but six hours' rising time was impractical. I needed a different method, so I contacted Dan Lepard, the baker, who has some radical bread-making techniques.

Embracing the unconventional

Dan's dough was even stickier and kneading was minimal. He believes it is hydration of the water with the flour over a period of time, rather than kneading, that activates the gluten to produce a stretchy, resilient dough. I tried a variation of Dan's method with an adaptation of Ursula's recipe, including her idea of mixing in semolina to enrich and strengthen the dough. Despite a short rising time and hardly any kneading, the dough had great texture and flavour, and was golden and crunchy from the semolina, but it wasn't thin enough. It just kept bouncing back as I rolled it out. I pulled it, prodded it, even tried throwing it up in the air – nothing helped – until I recalled that Dan oils the work surface first. Immediately it rolled out like a dream.

1 Mix the dough ingredients with your hands. It should feel very sticky.

Sorting out the topping

The topping ingredients for a Margherita pizza mirror the colours of the Italian flag – green, red and white from the basil, tomatoes and mozzarella. 'It's about balance,' Ursula said. 'You shouldn't taste one ingredient more than the others.' Then officialdom crept in again. 'The sauce should officially be smooth so it spreads easily,' she added. 'You could make a cooked sauce and purée it, or use passata and ladle it on – convenient, but lacking flavour.' I made up a cooked sauce and decided to keep it chunky. It tasted good, but should I have puréed it? Anna Venturi came up with another solution. 'Just use undressed tomatoes straight from the tin, there's no need to cook with onion.' I loved the speed and freshness of this topping, but missed the flavours of my cooked version. So I chopped in some garlic, squirted in a bit of tomato purée, and had flavour as well as speed. Ursula had another trick: 'Always hide the basil under the mozzarella to protect and keep its flavour.' She also told me that the government guidelines allow only the use of buffalo mozzarella. This was one ruling I was happy to comply with. Grating the cheese meant it could be evenly distributed, though slightly messy to do, so I tried ripping it, and preferred the definition this gave.

2 Snip the drained tomatoes into small pieces with scissors.

Getting a crisp crust

Without a wood-burning oven, how could I get an authentic crisp, dark crust? 'The reason a pizza comes out so crisp from a wood-burning oven,' said Anna, 'is that the oven is closed with a wooden door, then sealed, making it completely dry.' Intensity of heat helped give authenticity in my domestic oven, as long as the dough was really thin. When thicker, the cheese burnt before the dough had time to cook. Now I had the oven temperature and dough just right, the base was cooking quickly and evenly without having to heat the baking sheet

3 Drizzle with a little olive oil before baking.

first and, sprinkling semolina on the sheet helped to stop the dough sticking. 'The semolina acts like ball bearings,' Ursula told me, 'so the pizza just rolls off.' As my last test glided effortlessly off, I knew that my unconventional methods would never win me official *pizzaiola* status, but they will encourage me to make pizza more often.

The recipe

Makes 2 pizzas
(each serves 2)

Ready in about 1¾ hrs, including rising times

Fairly easy

What you need
For the pizza dough
350g/12oz strong white flour
25g/1oz coarse semolina, plus extra for sprinkling
1½ tsp salt, preferably fine sea salt
7g packet fast-action (also called easy-blend) dried yeast
1 tbsp olive oil (not extra-virgin), plus extra for drizzling
275ml/9fl oz tepid water

For the topping
400g can plum tomatoes
2 plump garlic cloves, finely chopped
2 tbsp tomato purée
2 balls buffalo mozzarella, (about 140g each)
2 small handfuls of fresh basil leaves, roughly torn
Parmesan shavings and rocket, to serve

Can be frozen

1. In a bowl, mix the flour, semolina, salt and yeast. Make a dip in the middle, pour in the oil and water, then stir and squeeze everything together (hands are easiest for this). The dough should feel very sticky. When it is well mixed, cover and leave for 15 minutes.
2. Tip the dough on to a lightly oiled work surface and rub your hands and the inside of the bowl with oil. Knead the dough about 12 times only, giving it a quarter turn each time you knead. Tuck the ends under so it is the shape of a ball and lay it in the bowl, seam-side down. Cover and leave for 10 minutes. Repeat the kneading and leaving for 10 minutes again, then knead and leave for 15 minutes, oiling the surface and your hands each time.
3. In between kneadings make the sauce for the topping. Drain the tomatoes and tip them into a bowl. Snip them into small pieces with scissors. Stir in the garlic, tomato purée and seasoning. Set aside. Brush a baking sheet with oil and sprinkle with a little semolina. Heat the oven to 240°C/fan 220°C/Gas 9.
4. When the dough is ready, cut it in half and put one half onto a lightly floured surface. Knead 4–5 times to squash out any air bubbles, then roll it out. At the point where it just keeps springing back, brush off the flour from the work surface and rub on a little oil. This makes it easier to roll. Continue to roll out until you have a 28cm/11in circle, pulling it into shape as well. Lift it onto the baking sheet (it's easier if you drape it over a rolling pin).
5. Drain the mozzarella, then pat dry with kitchen paper. Brush the dough with olive oil, then spread half the sauce over, almost up to the edge. Scatter over half the basil, then tear up one mozzarella ball and scatter it over the basil. Grind over black pepper and drizzle with a little oil. Bake for 12–15 minutes, until the topping is bubbling and the dough is going brown. Repeat with the remaining dough and toppings. To serve, scatter with Parmesan shavings, rocket leaves and drizzle with oil.

5

BEST-EVER SIDE ORDERS AND SAUCES

Hollandaise Sauce

Sauces can be scary. So many things can go wrong, especially with the classic French ones that often rely on skilled techniques and scientific know-how. But that's why I love hollandaise. OK, it's fattening – there's not much else in there apart from egg yolks and butter – and it can curdle, separate and even end up as thick and lumpy as mashed potato, or as thin and runny as an oil slick. Once in a while, however, it's a delightful treat, and best of all there's a foolproof modern version that even top chefs have been known to resort to, which is all made in a matter of minutes in the food processor. Though aware of this speedy version when I began testing, I firmly believed that after all my experimenting, the time-consuming classic version would win the contest, and for a while I wasn't to be persuaded otherwise.

Discovering the possibilities

I referred to the cookbooks of such culinary dignitaries as Jane Grigson, Robert Carrier, Michel Roux, Delia Smith, Gary Rhodes, Raymond Blanc and Rick Stein. I was after a light, slightly airy and voluptuous sauce, with as much stability as possible. Here's how their classical recipes varied: the number of egg yolks to butter (anything from 2–4 using 225–250g butter); the type of butter – salted and unsalted – and no other specifications, apart from Jane Grigson who mentioned French Isigny when she wrote, 'Sometimes it (hollandaise) is called sauce Isigny, a genuflection to the home town of France's best butter'; flavourings – competition emerged between the use of lemon juice or white wine vinegar as the favoured choice of acidity used to cut the richness (though vinegar probably had the winning edge, I would try both). Most used white pepper, some ground it, some left it whole. Extra flavourings were bay, mace, cayenne, mustard, shallot and tarragon (not all together, as subtlety seemed to be the key). The final variation was the method of making. Some started with a reduction of the acid with varying amounts of water, others added it neat. When it came to amalgamating the egg yolks and butter, some did this in a bain marie or directly in a pan. Butter was clarified or not, melted or not, added on or off the heat. Jane Grigson used a wooden spoon to stir, Robert Carrier preferred a wire whisk, while Raymond Blanc chose the electric whisk.

Taking the classical route

After trying half a dozen different classical versions, I could see both problems and solutions. As I glanced down the line of bowls containing my experiments, I was struck by how different they looked. When

I used a wire whisk rather than a wooden spoon, the sauce was paler, lighter. If made in a pan, rather than over the more gentle bain marie, it was easier to overcook and scramble the sauce. Even over the bain marie, great care had to be taken that the bowl over the water did not overheat. At one point I ran out of eggs and nipped to the local shop. The eggs were cheap and the sauce lacked the golden glow of the organic ones I'd been using. Although all the recipes were different at this stage, there were several contenders for best, and I was pretty sure I wouldn't improve on them. What struck me most, however, was the time it took to make this sauce – around three quarters of an hour seems impractical for most of us. Clarifying the butter is a tedious procedure in which you melt it and pour the golden liquid into a fresh jug, discarding the milky solids at the bottom, but it did improve the flavour. To cut corners, I grabbed the food processor.

1 Strain the vinegar mixture into a jug.

Breaking with tradition

My first attempt, done in a hurry, was disappointing. It was quick; five minutes as the machine did all the work, but the sauce was runny. I put it down to 'more haste, less speed', as my second go was different again. This time I heated the water and lemon juice to be added to the egg yolks in the food processor, and took longer adding the butter (which was very hot). It was miraculous, a silky smooth-textured sauce in under 10 minutes but the taste just wasn't right. My food processor version felt flat. Yes the texture was good, but it needed an injection of flavour.

2 Slowly add the butter, drop by drop.

Mixing classic and contemporary

I decided to blend the traditional with new by combining the flavoured reduction (made with peppercorns, bay, white wine vinegar and water) with the food processor technique. Straight away, I felt I was on to a winner, and by adding a little lemon juice right at the end rather than earlier, the flavour came through crisply and cleanly. There was one more thing I wanted to check – the butter – so I whizzed up more batches using different types. Because butter is the main ingredient, I expected a huge difference in the taste between a cheap salted butter compared with the French Isigny or other more expensive ones. There wasn't really, though the French semi or unsalted had the edge. If the butter is salted, don't add extra salt until you've finished and tasted the sauce, or it can end up too salty. Another tip to improve flavour is to stop adding the melted butter when you reach the milky white solids at the bottom of the pan, a short cut to clarifying the butter.

3 Add the lemon juice at the end, while the sauce is still warm.

Last-minute discoveries

Like many sauces, hollandaise doesn't benefit from hanging around. However, I found the food processor version a lot more stable than the classical, and I could keep it warm for about half an hour after making. I now had my ultimate hollandaise, or so I thought. It then occurred to me that I'd been using four egg yolks with all my tests. What if I added fewer? I made one more sauce with three egg yolks this time and an extra tablespoon of hot water with the reduction, which made it lighter, more voluptuous. As I dipped an asparagus spear into it to scoop up a mouthful, I knew this was the ultimate.

The recipe

Serves 4
(makes 225ml/8fl oz)

Ready in 20–25 minutes

Easy

What you need

3 egg yolks, preferably organic
½ tsp white peppercorns
250g pack butter, unsalted or semi-salted
3 tbsp white wine vinegar
1 bay leaf
about ½ tsp lemon juice, or to taste

1 Drop the egg yolks into a food processor. If you are using unsalted butter, add a pinch of salt (preferably sea salt), otherwise leave it out for now. Pulse the egg yolks just until they have broken down, then turn off the machine.

2 Roughly crush the peppercorns using a pestle and mortar (or a bowl and the end of a rolling pin). Cut the butter into big pieces, drop them into a medium pan and melt over a low heat. At the same time, pour the wine vinegar into a small pan with 3 tablespoons of water, the peppercorns and the bay leaf. Simmer for a few minutes only until the mixture has reduced to 2 tablespoons (keep watching, as the liquid can disappear quickly). Add 1 tablespoon of boiling water, then strain this mixture into a jug. By now the butter should be just starting to bubble so take it off the heat and skim off any frothy scum.

3 At this point you want both the butter and the wine vinegar reduction to be hot but not boiling. Turn on the food processor and pour in the reduction in a steady stream. When it's all added, stop the processor. Next, with the processor running, slowly add the butter, drop by drop. You can speed up towards the end, but for now it's best to do it slowly, so it blends in with the egg yolks (it will look quite runny until the last of the butter goes in).

4 When nearly all the butter has been added, you will notice a little pool of milky mixture in the bottom of the pan. These are the milk solids, so don't add, leave them behind in the pan.

5 While the sauce is still warm, taste and adjust the salt and add the lemon juice. Quickly scoop it out of the machine and into your warmed serving bowl. Serve straight away, or if you want to keep it warm, fill a small heatproof bowl with boiling water, tip out the water, pour in the hollandaise, then cover with cling film. It will keep for up to 20 minutes.

Pesto

If you have never made your own pesto, I urge you to have a go. I became a convert to the real thing while attending a cooking school in Tuscany, run by Canadian-based chef Umberto Menghi. Food writers Claudia Roden and Valentina Harris are both supporters of homemade too. 'When you make it at home it always tastes less sour,' said Valentina. 'There's nothing wrong with the jar stuff, but it takes that lovely sweetness away.' Pesto comes from the coastal region of Liguria, an area of rough mountainous terrain where herbs thrive. 'They can be grown close together, tucked into terraces or window boxes or on tiny plots of land,' Valentina told me.

Tradition versus convenience

Pounding pesto the traditional way using a pestle and mortar is wonderfully therapeutic, but quite hard work, and I found little difference in the end result whether done this way or in a machine. Claudia Roden gave me permission to take the easy route. 'Some say it is better to pound, and if I have time I do, but when I was shown how to make pesto in Liguria they used a blender, so I feel entitled to as well.'

Concentrating colour and taste

There are many versions of pesto, which can include walnuts, almonds, bread, even tomatoes. However, I would stick with the classic ingredients of garlic, pine nuts, basil, olive oil and Parmesan. When Valentina divulged a handy tip, I did diversify slightly. 'The Italian trick is to get a really good green and up the chlorophyll by adding spinach or parsley,' she explained. This immediately reminded me of the pesto I had made in Italy that had replaced some of the basil with parsley. I adjusted the recipe accordingly. The fragrance and taste of the basil remained; parsley just made everything fresher and lighter. I had been whizzing the ingredients to a super-smooth paste, until I recalled Valentina's advice, 'the greatest danger is to overwork the basil so it doesn't taste of basil. It's a delicate plant so needs to be treated as such.' When I whizzed less furiously I much preferred the slight chunkiness I got, especially from the cheese and nuts.

Lots of Italian advice

Valentina then explained how she liked to get a balance between all the different elements. 'There is an argument over the cheese and garlic: some say to use half Pecorino, half Parmesan; some say all Pecorino; some say all Parmesan. In Italy we make ours a lot less garlicky than in

England. Then there's the basil. Depending on its fragrance I may lower or up the amount. You need to keep tasting.' After upping and lowering amounts of all the ingredients, I came up with a balance I was happy with, but the type of oil was affecting the consistency. Extra-virgin was making it too thick. I sought Valentina's advice. 'Use a light one that doesn't have an overpowering pepperiness,' she advised. This immediately thinned things out. With the recipe now sorted, I passed it to a friend to try. Her verdict? 'I'll never be able to eat it from a jar again,' she said, 'it's nothing like the real thing.'

The recipe

Makes about 300ml/½ pint

Ready in
about 10–15 minutes

Easy

What you need
85g/3oz Parmesan
2 garlic cloves
85g/3oz pine nuts
25g packet fresh basil
20g packet fresh flat-leaf parsley
125ml/4fl oz good-quality olive oil, preferably Ligurian

Can be frozen (either in ice cube trays or a small plastic freezer bag)

How to store
This pesto keeps in the fridge for up to a week. Keep it fresh by making sure it is topped up and covered all the time with a thin layer of olive oil.

1 Cut the cheese into small cubes and roughly chop the garlic. Drop the cheese, garlic and pine nuts into a food processor. Pluck the leaves of basil and parsley from their stems, and drop these in too (discard the stems). Whizz until everything is fairly coarsely chopped.
2 With the machine running, slowly pour in the oil until you get a soft green mixture that is not too oily. It's quite good if the paste isn't completely smooth and you have a few pieces of nuts and cheese. Taste and adjust with salt and pepper if needed, though the cheese will have a lot of salt anyway.

Hummus

Shop-bought hummus tastes fine, is convenient and readily available. So why spend time creating a more time-consuming version? As food writer Claudia Roden pointed out, it would be much tastier if I made my own. Author Ghillie Başan (who has lived and worked in the Middle East and Turkey) agreed. 'It's very easy to make in the blender – then you can play around with it, make it more lemony, spicy and refreshing.'

Chickpea taste test

I could make the hummus traditionally by pounding dried, cooked chickpeas using a pestle and mortar or I could eliminate the hard work by quickly whizzing canned chickpeas in a blender. I tried both. Removing the skins from the dried cooked chickpeas made them easier to bash but already this was proving too labour-intensive. A blender was easier, but was the overnight soaking and 1½ hours' cooking time worth it? I then did a much quicker test using canned chickpeas and a blender. As Ghillie had warned me that canned ones could taste metallic, I decided to simmer the chickpeas briefly with the garlic, which not only took away any metallic taste, it also softened the powerful taste of raw garlic I had been getting. Although the colour of the canned version was slightly duller, the tasters were unable to detect a difference in flavour between that and the one made with dried chick peas.

Balancing flavours

I was happy with the speedy method, but needed to inject more flavour. There were several options. I had always thought tahini (sesame seed paste) was an essential ingredient for hummus, but both Claudia and Ghillie told me it is often omitted in the Turkish version. I found a recipe using sesame oil, but preferred tahini as it improved both taste and texture. However, when too much went in, the hummus tasted bitter. Cumin again was optional, and it could be toasted or not. I toasted then ground the seeds and liked the spicy edge it introduced. The balance of lemon juice and garlic was important, and easy to adjust at the end to suit personal preferences.

A special topping to finish

Claudia had explained how hummus is softer and creamier in Middle Eastern countries. In search of this texture I dropped in some yogurt (a tip from Ghillie) which helped, but not enough. I then noticed the liquid the chickpeas had been cooked in and poured in that. The whole texture changed to one of soft creaminess. I then looked for ways to finish it off. Claudia and Ghillie had told me of a hot fluffy version, using similar ingredients, which is topped with toasted pine nuts and chilli flakes and baked in the oven. I didn't want to bake the hummus, but decided to incorporate the topping idea for a contrasting crunch. My ultimate version was now not only loaded with flavour, it was as quick to make as to go out and buy.

The recipe

Makes about 400g/14oz (enough for 4 servings as a snack, more as a part of a meze)

Ready in 20 minutes

Easy

What you need

410g can chickpeas, preferably organic
3 garlic cloves, peeled and roughly chopped
½ tsp cumin seeds
juice of ½ lemon (2 tbsp)
2 tbsp tahini
2 tbsp natural yogurt
3 tbsp extra-virgin olive oil
toasted pine nuts, crushed dried chillies, chopped fresh parsley and extra-virgin olive oil, to garnish

Make-ahead tip
If making ahead, the hummus stiffens slightly as it chills, so beat well before using.

1 Tip the chickpeas into a sieve to drain, then put them in a small pan with the garlic cloves. Pour in enough water to cover, bring to a boil, then lower the heat and simmer for 5 minutes. Meanwhile, heat a small heavy-based pan, tip in the cumin seeds and heat for about a minute, just until they start to turn colour (they will start to smell fragrant when ready). Shake the pan every now and then so they don't burn and blacken. Grind them to a fine powder using a pestle and mortar.
2 Drain the chickpeas, reserving about 5 tablespoons of the liquid. Keep a few chickpeas back to use as garnish and tip the rest into a food processor or blender with the garlic and the reserved liquid. Process until smooth, then pour in the lemon juice and pulse again, scraping down the sides of the processor occasionally. Now to get it creamy: add the tahini, yogurt and oil with the cumin and some salt to season and pulse again. The hummus should be soft and thickly pourable. Leave to cool, then adjust with lemon and salt if necessary to suit your own taste. It will keep in the fridge for up to 4 days.
3 To serve, spoon the hummus into a serving bowl, give it a swirl, then scatter over the reserved chickpeas, pine nuts, a sprinkling of dried chillies, chopped parsley and a drizzle of oil.

Ratatouille

Ratatouille means so much more to me now than a mere 'vegetable stew'. Before working on this recipe, I never paid enough attention to the individuality of the ingredients, recklessly slicing up everything far too large, then allowing it all to simmer away for far too long so you couldn't distinguish one vegetable from another, but not any more. After conversations with chefs Alex Mackay and Shaun Hill, the way I make ratatouille has been revolutionised.

What is essential?

There are many interpretations of this recipe and, as Shaun Hill reminded me, 'this is a peasant dish that comes from a large area, so all have their own way of doing it.' As to its origin, Alex's idea was that it 'probably came about from using a glut of vegetables, when everything ripens together.' During research I discovered that the glut of basic vegetables called for remained pretty constant. Elizabeth David, for example, was very clear in her book *French Provincial Cooking* (Penguin Books) about which to include: 'aubergines, sweet peppers, onions, tomatoes, with courgettes sometimes being added and occasionally potatoes as well.' For her, garlic was optional, olive oil a must. Shaun Hill was quite relaxed about additions. 'I'm easy with celery and mushroom,' he said, but agreed, 'you do need all the main players.'

Improving the texture

What I was keen to overcome was the mushy stew I usually ended up with when I cooked all the vegetables together. At the suggestion of both Shaun and Alex, the first thing I did differently was to cook the tomatoes separately to make a sauce. The other vegetables would be added to this later. However, I wasn't cooking this in the south of France, so how could I achieve that characteristic sweetness? Shaun suggested I might get more flavour from tomatoes in a can or jar. I found, however, that if I picked out the reddest of the large tomatoes growing on the vine, and let them slowly break down into a sauce, by the time they were combined with the other vegetables, a natural sweetness occurred. In fact several tasters thought I had added sugar. Shaun and Alex both advised cutting the vegetables much smaller and more uniformly than I was used to doing. 'Cut the vegetables into chunks, roughly the same size,' Alex said, 'then when you take a forkful you will get a bit of everything.' As to the initial cooking of the peppers, aubergines and courgettes, it was suggested I cook them separately, to keep them fresh. This sounded fiddly but Alex reassured me. 'It's not

complicated. While the sauce simmers, you are frying the vegetables, then it all comes together.' It worked so well, I won't be doing it any other way now. Both colour, shape and texture of each vegetable was preserved, and the tomato sauce bound everything together in a colourful, juicy way.

Fine-tuning techniques

I had been salting the aubergines but, since ingredients have changed so much over the years, questioned whether it was really necessary. 'Not all agree, but I never salt aubergines,' Alex told me. 'The idea is you salt to get the bitter juices out, the salt opens the pores to draw out the moisture, then you wash them to get rid of the salt. So it defeats the purpose.' I immediately stopped salting. By fine-tuning the cooking times (which meant shortening them) then letting the vegetables mingle together with the tomato sauce, the ratatouille was now much fresher, and also wonderfully creamy from the aubergines.

A taste of Provençe

What it still needed was a touch of intrigue, some kind of subtle background flavouring. I wrapped a sprig of Provençal herbs, thyme and rosemary in a fresh bay leaf to bring a south-of-France fragrance to the sauce. But what else? Alex suggested dried orange zest, a very traditional flavouring for Provençal stews. I returned to Elizabeth David's book for

1 Wrap the thyme and rosemary in the bay leaf to make a bouquet garni, and tie up with non-coloured string.

2 Add the tomatoes and the bouquet garni to the onion and garlic and cook very gently.

3 Fry the peppers for about 5 minutes over a highish heat until just softened.

inspiration, and found she added crushed coriander seeds. To complement the seeds, I finished the dish off with a flourish of fresh coriander and a little parsley. This was as far removed from my mushy over-stewed version as I could ever have hoped for.

The recipe

Serves 4

Ready in about 1¼ hours

Easy

What you need

2 medium onions
5–6 large tomatoes (about 450g/1lb), preferably vine-ripened, chopped
bunch of fresh thyme
fresh sprig of rosemary
1 bay leaf
2 tbsp olive oil, plus 100ml/3½fl oz and extra for drizzling
4 garlic cloves, finely chopped
2 red peppers
3 medium courgettes
1 large aubergine
1½ tsp coriander seeds, crushed
fresh coriander and parsley to finish
crusty French bread, to serve

Can be frozen

1 Make the tomato sauce first. Chop the onions (not too finely). Quarter the tomatoes and cut out their cores. Roughly chop the tomatoes. Wrap the thyme and rosemary in the bay leaf to make a bouquet garni, and tie up with non-coloured string.

2 Heat the 2 tablespoons of oil and fry the onion and garlic in a wok or deep frying pan, until soft but not coloured, stirring occasionally (you sweat rather than fry them), for about 12–15 minutes. Add the tomatoes and the bouquet garni and cook very gently, uncovered, for about 20–25 minutes until saucy, giving the occasional stir.

3 While the sauce is simmering, prepare the rest of the vegetables. Remove the cores and seeds from the peppers and cut them into 2.5cm/1in pieces. Cut the courgettes and aubergine into the same size pieces as the peppers.

4 Heat one third of the remaining 100ml/3½ fl oz oil in a frying pan and fry the peppers for about 5 minutes over a highish heat until just softened and tinged brown, stirring occasionally. Tip them out into a bowl or onto a plate, add another third of the oil to the frying pan and fry the aubergines in the same way for 5 minutes. Don't be tempted to add more oil if they look dry as they first soak up the oil, just keep stirring. Tip them onto the peppers. Add the rest of the oil and fry the courgettes for 5 minutes until golden, stirring often. Tip into the bowl.

5 Stir these vegetables into the tomato sauce with the crushed coriander, cover and simmer on a gentle murmur for about 15 minutes until all the vegetables are soft and tender but not breaking up. Season to taste. Throw in some freshly chopped coriander and parsley to serve and drizzle with olive oil to finish. Eat with chunks of crusty French bread to mop up the juices.

Serving suggestions

Ratatouille is good on its own, as a side dish, or served with a piece of pan-fried or roast chicken or fish on top. It's even good cold, and if left for a day or two the flavours develop all the more.

Spiced Red Cabbage

Taking a fresh look at this traditional Scandinavian Christmas dish has made me realise how predictable I had become when making it. I loved the sweet and sour spiciness of the flavourings I usually used, but felt everything needed reconsidering and fine-tuning. Also, I needed to decide whether cooking it on top of the stove or in the oven would be best for preserving both texture and colour. I came across many recipes similar to mine with as many ingredients – chunks of apple and onion, bacon, raisins, sugar, orange zest, cinnamon, cloves and a splash of vinegar and orange juice or red wine. Despite finding ones that introduced new ideas such as chillies and herbs instead of sugar and spice, I wanted to keep the Christmassy flavours, but concentrate them so they would bring the cabbage together in a glossy, flavoursome juiciness. So, how could this be achieved?

Taking out – putting back in

After a conversation with chef Shaun Hill I decided that simplicity was the way to go. For him, apples were definitely out, he disliked the texture of them with the cabbage. 'I add orange juice and red wine rather than apples. I also add onion, sugar, salt and pepper and cinnamon. That's all.' So for my first test, I pruned the recipe right down. Out went the bacon, raisins, even the apples. I didn't miss those chunky bits at all, having often thought that their texture fought with the shredded cabbage. Hoping to simplify things even further, I just tipped everything into the pan and let it all simmer away. Although I had added orange juice, I missed the fresh apple taste and, through speed of cooking, had ended up with a rather bland cabbage dish sitting in runny liquid. I quickly made some more adjustments. Fragrant star anise took the place of overpowering cloves, apple juice replaced orange, and dried cranberries replaced apple chunks (this brought back the fruity taste I was missing in a more balanced way). After playing around with the amount of sugar so it wasn't too sweet, I decided that a mixture of light muscovado with redcurrant jelly gave a combined subtle sweetness and glossiness, while red wine vinegar put the sweet-sour kick back in.

Cooking it differently

I now needed to adjust the cooking method. To create a flavoursome, syrupy base, I fried whole spices, caramelised the sugar and sizzled the apple juice with the onion before the cabbage was introduced to it. Longer cooking gave more time for the cabbage to take on the flavours, but I still wanted to try braising it in the oven. This proved more gentle;

the cabbage was more moist, texture and colour were left intact and the whole thing was enveloped with a spicy taste that was no longer predictable. I certainly won't be saving this dish just for Christmas.

The recipe

Serves 6

Ready in about 1 hour 20 minutes (includes 1 hour in the oven)

Easy

What you need

1 small red cabbage, about 900g/2lb
85g/3oz butter
1 medium onion, halved lengthways and thinly sliced
3 star anise
1 cinnamon stick, snapped in half
3 tbsp light muscovado sugar
3 tbsp red wine vinegar
125ml/4fl oz pure apple juice, a cloudy one that has good flavour
100g/4oz dried cranberries
1 rounded tbsp redcurrant jelly (with added port is good)

Can be frozen

Using fresh cranberries
Stir them into the cabbage for the last 15 minutes of cooking time in the oven.

1 Heat the oven to 160°C/fan 140°C/Gas 3. Quarter the cabbage, cut out the hard white core from each piece, then slice the cabbage thinly (with a knife or in the food processor). Melt the butter in a large deep sauté pan or saucepan, add the onion and cook for 5 minutes or so until softened and buttery, but not browned, stirring occasionally.

2 Drop in the star anise and cinnamon and fry, stirring, for a minute to release their flavours. Stir in the sugar to dissolve and caramelise it slightly. Pour in the red wine vinegar, let it sizzle, then add the apple juice so it sizzles too. Tip in the cranberries and simmer for a couple of minutes to plump them up. Stir in the redcurrant jelly until it has dissolved. The mixture should be slightly syrupy.

3 Add the cabbage, give it all a good stir, then simmer for 2 minutes, stirring occasionally so everything is shiny. Transfer the cabbage mix to an ovenproof dish. Cover with a lid (or tightly with foil if the dish doesn't have one) and braise in the oven for about an hour, or until the cabbage is tender, but still has a slight crunch with enough glossy liquid to coat it. Season as you like it with salt and pepper, stir, and remove the whole spices before serving. Goes well with game, chicken, pork and turkey.

Make-ahead tip
Can be made a day ahead, in fact it's even better. Just reheat gently in a large pan, or in the microwave.

Yorkshire Puddings

I've gained a lot of respect for Yorkshire puddings. What ingenious, yet practical culinary containers they are, and made with just four ingredients. However, it's amazing what a few ingredients can get up to once they are in the oven. I was reminded of its humble beginnings by Yorkshire-born Anne Willan who spoke of them being served at the start of a meal to take the edge off appetites, so people ate less of the expensive meat. She recalled one of her uncles who always insisted on eating a couple of crispy puddings dowsed with gravy as a first course. When I called chef Stephen Jackson, whose restaurant The Weaver's Shed in West Yorkshire has been serving Yorkshire puddings for over 30 years, he told me of guests who used to order theirs dry, with just a little salt and pepper and a splash of vinegar for diversion. The Yorkshire pudding is steeped in tradition, but I was to discover that it's a fickle recipe; sometimes it works, sometimes it doesn't and many other people I spoke to agreed. It was when I read in Jane Grigson's *English Food* (Penguin) that a Chinese man once won a Yorkshire pudding contest in Leeds, that I decided to question tradition. Mr Tin Sung Chan's approach had apparently been most unconventional, yet the *Guardian* reporter who covered the contest noted, 'his pudding swelled to the height of a Coronation crown.'

Seeking expert advice

To create my own Yorkshires with tall, crispy sides, slightly soft bottoms and airy interiors, I went to see how sous chef Andy Cook made them for Sunday lunch at Gordon Ramsay's at Claridge's, London. I liked his unusual approach. Most traditional recipes call for sifting the flour into a bowl, making a well to beat the eggs in, then slowly adding the milk. Andy did it differently. He whisked eggs (plus an egg white) with a balloon whisk, and gradually beat in unsifted, unmeasured flour until the batter looked like melted white chocolate. Milk and water were also added unmeasured, until it poured like double cream. The Yorkshires rose with gusto, dainty, crisp and light. Had I already discovered the ultimate recipe?

Testing begins

Back in the test kitchen and after talking to more chefs and cooks, I found a hotbed of controversy, as there were still many questions to answer. Type of flour, number of eggs, milk on its own or with water, mixing method, consistency of batter, the oven temperature, type of tin, type of fat – everything seemed up for grabs. I experimented first with

different mixing methods. I tried Jamie Oliver's throw-everything-into-a-bowl-and-give-it-a-vigorous-beat-style. So easy, and with an extra egg the mixture billowed up, making a softer, gutsy Yorkshire, but it lacked crispness. I tried traditional methods, then Andy's recipe with Jamie's mixing, but finally decided it was the addition of the egg white with Andy's unconventional mixing method that was the right direction.

1 As you whisk, the mixture thickens to resemble a sloppy paste.

Debunking some myths

Most chefs and cooks leave their batter to stand but timings vary wildly, and is it really necessary? Yorkshire chef Brian Turner swears by leaving the batter for 30 minutes. Stephen Jackson follows his father's tip: mix the batter early in the morning and 'its good and ready by lunchtime'. I tried, even left it overnight, but found it made little difference. *Delia Smith's Winter Collection* (BBC Books) agrees: 'It's rumoured that batter left to stand is better, but I have found no foundation for this.' I was told of secret ingredients being added like ale, even snow. Brian Turner mixes in a spoonful of malt vinegar. 'I've no idea why,' he confessed, 'that's what my Gran did so I daren't leave it out.' I did, and all was fine.

2 When done, the batter should look just a bit thinner than double cream.

Hot fat, hot tin, hot oven

As my experiments continued I was puzzled; some batches blew up like balloons, others looked deflated. Though I'd now settled on the recipe – milk mixed with a little water, eggs plus an egg white, definitely plain flour – and preferred individual Yorkshires over one big one, the batter was not behaving consistently. My attention turned to the fat and the tin. The fat didn't affect the finished result, only the flavour; oil gave the mildest, goose fat (from a tin) or beef dripping the best. The one thing everyone agreed on, however, was that if the fat's smoking hot, and you use a generous amount, the rise is more assured. So I took the non-stick tray and experimented with different oven temperatures. It needed to be high, but when too hot the puddings over-browned before they cooked through, not hot enough and the dramatic rise was lost. Starting the heat high, then lowering it was working best, but I was still a victim of inconsistency.

3 As the batter is poured into the hot fat, it should start to sizzle around the edges.

Some last-minute discoveries

By now I was running out of tins and patience. Orlando Murrin, Editorial Director of *BBC Good Food Magazine*, swears by his flexible muffin pans, but they're meant to be used without fat. Finally I grabbed a cheap metal tin, it wasn't non-stick and quite thin. Up until now I'd used a conventional oven so I had nothing to lose by switching to fan.

Amazingly, the batter rose majestically and evenly but was it the cheap old tin or the snazzy new oven? It was both, but above all, getting the fat hot, using a fan oven, not opening the door too early, keeping a steady 200°C, all worked a treat, even using the thicker non-stick tray. I had created my ultimate Yorkshire puddings with a blend of old-fashioned know-how and modern technology.

The recipe

Makes 8

Ready in 40–50 minutes

Easy

What you need

goose fat, or beef dripping or sunflower oil
2 eggs, preferably organic
1 egg white
115g/4oz plain flour mixed with ¼ tsp salt
175ml/6fl oz full-fat milk
2 x 4-hole Yorkshire pudding trays

Can be frozen

1 Heat the oven to 220°C/fan 200°C/Gas 7. Fan oven is best, preheated. (If you're cooking a roast, cook the Yorkshires while the meat is resting.) Spoon a scant tablespoon of beef dripping, goose fat or oil into each hole of the Yorkshire pudding tray (there is enough batter for two trays). When the oven is up to temperature, put the trays in and leave for 15 minutes for the fat to get really hot.

2 Meanwhile, crack the whole eggs and the egg white into a large bowl. Beat together with a balloon whisk until well combined. Start to add the flour, a couple of spoonfuls at a time, beating well with the whisk as you go to keep the lumps at bay and the mixture smooth. You will see the mixture start to thicken and it will look like a sloppy paste.

3 When all the flour has been added, measure the milk in a jug and make it up to 225ml/8fl oz with water, then begin gradually to pour in the liquid, again a little at a time, whisking as you go, until it is smooth. It should now look just a bit thinner than double cream. Pour the batter back into the jug.

4 Carefully lift the tin of hot fat out of the oven, using oven gloves, and quickly pour a little batter into each tin, in a circular movement, so each is three quarters full. The batter should start to sizzle in the hot fat around the edges as it is poured in. Bake for 15–20 minutes until the Yorkshires are tall, golden, puffed and crisp on the sides. Pour off any excess fat and serve with your favourite roast.

Storage tip

Once cooled they can be frozen. Reheat from frozen at 180°C/fan 160°C/Gas 4 for 4–5 minutes.

Roast Potatoes

There's nothing difficult about roasting a few potatoes, is there? You just peel, chop, tip them into a pan, toss in a bit of oil (that's 10 minutes' work maximum), then you roast them for about an hour while you get on with something else. So when Kathryn Race of the British Potato Council told me that frozen roast potatoes are the best-selling frozen potato product from the supermarket, I wondered why. My first guess was that people adore them. Secondly, if you are after that perfectly golden, crisp and crunchy outside with a soft, fluffy inside, roasting potatoes isn't at all straightforward. There's the type of potato to consider. Then, should you parboil, and if so, for how long? Also there's the choice of fat, type of roasting tin, when to add salt, not to mention the heat of the oven.

Choosing the right potato

'Getting the right variety is key,' said Kathryn. 'There are two basic types: waxy, which has a firmer texture so keeps its shape more, and floury, which is softer and breaks down more easily. For roasting you want a floury texture, but not so floury that the potato ends up as mash. Nor should it be too waxy or you won't get that nice fluffiness.' I began by roasting different varieties. Marfona and Estima, traditionally used for baking, didn't go particularly crisp, and the inside texture was far too soft. Romano was marginally better, but the outside skins were too thin and the insides not floury enough. Desirée turned dark golden, almost caramelised, so looked remarkably crisp, but as one taster commented, 'They taste like soggy, sweet chips.' I knew Desirée was perfectly capable of creating a good roast potato, but why not on the day I tried? And why was it so sweet?

A chef's view

I went to see Stuart Gillies, head chef and business partner of Gordon Ramsay at Boxwood Café in London. His style of cooking is very English, very seasonal, and he is passionate about roast potatoes. In his opinion, the texture of Maris Piper is perfect for roasting. 'It is the most consistent variety all year round, and never goes powdery, as a King Edward can. Being a natural product,' Stuart explained, 'the potato is susceptible to change, as its sugar and starch content varies depending on the time of year, which is why you often get a different result from one season to the next.' That explained my sweetly caramelised Desirée. I have often favoured King Edward, so wasn't at all surprised by how well it roasted. It gave me a gutsy potato that darkened quickly, but

I agreed with Stuart that it seemed a bit powdery. I was definitely getting the best, most consistent results from the Maris Piper. It kept its shape, didn't shrink or break up, had the floury texture I was after without being powdery, plus an added creaminess, and it also turned the most glorious amber brown.

Getting crisp outsides

Having narrowed down the potato variety, I concentrated on getting a really crisp crust that would give contrast to the fluffy, floury interior. I roasted potatoes from raw, but they stuck. Cooking from raw also meant I couldn't 'rough them up' prior to roasting. This technique is often recommended as a way to make the outsides even crisper, done after parboiling either by scratching them all over with a fork (fiddly), or shaking them around in the pan or colander. So I tried parboiling for different lengths of time. It was easy to overcook the potatoes at this stage, but I knew it was an important step worth pursuing, and Stuart explained why. 'Parboiling takes off the excess starch and seals the outside of the potato, which stops it sticking to the tin,' he said. Unlike many recipes that suggest anything from 4 to 10 minutes for this process, Stuart parboils for 2 minutes maximum. I tried this and loved the way it kept the shape of the potato intact. Stuart also advised heating the roasting tin and the oil or fat. This got the potatoes off to a flying start and helped reduce the roasting time. Kathryn had also told me about the importance of a hot tin and hot fat. 'If the potatoes go into hot fat they will soak up less of it than if they go into cold fat,' she said, 'which means they will crisp up better.' My tests verified this, but I was after even more crispness, so I tried lightly flouring the potatoes after parboiling, a trick Gary Rhodes uses. This was no extra work and I couldn't help but be impressed by the crisp coating it gave. The potatoes had been getting crisp without it, but not as much, nor did they stay crisp for as long. Flouring also eliminated the need for roughing up, but I still preferred to do this for the texture it gave.

Fine tuning

I had been using olive oil for roasting as it can take very high temperatures without burning, as can sunflower or groundnut oil (though blander in taste). However, for a luxurious flavour, you can't beat goose or duck fat – well worth getting for special occasions. As for the roasting tin, it must be sturdy and big enough to take the potatoes in one layer. If overcrowded, the potatoes end up stewed rather than roasted. As long as you parboil the potatoes, and put them into a hot tin with hot fat, they shouldn't stick. For the oven temperature, a steady

1 Peel and cut the potatoes into even-sized pieces.

2 Drain then shake the potatoes a few times in a colander to fluff up the outsides.

3 Turn and roll the potatoes in the hot fat so they are coated all over.

200°C/fan 180°C/Gas 6 proved the most effective and practical, being the temperature usually used to roast a joint. Food writer Ruth Watson offered one final piece of advice: 'roast potatoes will *not* tolerate hanging around,' she said adamantly. 'They just get tough and boring.' With my recipe for crisp, fluffy roast potatoes now all sorted, next time I roast a few it won't be difficult at all, whatever the time of year.

The recipe

Serves 4

Ready in about an hour

Easy

What you need
1kg/2lb 4oz Maris Piper potatoes
100g/4oz goose or duck fat (for a luxurious taste), or 100ml/3½fl oz olive oil
2 tsp flour

Tips from chef Stuart Gillies
- To get ahead, parboil the potatoes and leave them to cool so they are quick to roast when you are ready. They will never be as good if you completely roast them ahead then re-heat.
- If serving with a joint, the potatoes will become crisper if you cook them in their own tin rather than around the meat, in the hottest part of the oven.

1 Put a roasting tin in the oven (one big enough to take the potatoes in a single layer) and heat the oven to 200°C/fan 180°C/Gas 6. Peel the potatoes and cut each into 4 even-sized pieces if they are medium size, 2–3 if smaller (5cm/2in pieces). Drop the potatoes into a large pan and pour in enough water to barely cover them. Add salt, then wait for the water to boil. As soon as the water reaches a full rolling boil, lower the heat, put your timer on and simmer the potatoes uncovered, reasonably vigorously, for 2 minutes. Meanwhile, put your choice of fat into the hot roasting tin and heat it in the oven for a few minutes, so it's really hot.

2 Drain the potatoes in a colander. Now it's time to rough them up a bit. Shake the colander back and forth a few times to fluff up the outsides. Sprinkle with the flour, and give another shake so they are evenly and thinly coated. Carefully put the potatoes into the hot fat (they will sizzle as they go in) then turn and roll them around so they are coated all over. Spread them in a single layer, making sure they have plenty of room.

3 Roast the potatoes for 15 minutes, then take them out of the oven and turn them over. Roast for another 15 minutes and turn them over again. Put them back in the oven for another 10–20 minutes, or however long it takes to get them really golden and crisp. The colouring will not be even, which is what you want. Scatter with salt and serve immediately.

Extra flavours
For another flavour dimension, cut a garlic bulb in half widthways (peel on) and tuck it among the potatoes at the end of step 2, along with a bunch of thyme or rosemary, or both.

Gratin Dauphinois

At first I thought I had it easy with this recipe. My challenge was a simple classic creamy potato gratin – very few ingredients, and not too many variables. I'd have this one sorted relatively quickly, but when even the correct name of the dish sparked off a ferocious argument, I knew I was mistaken. The choices came thick and fast – what type of potato should I use, should the slices be soaked first, should I add cheese or not, should the liquid be cream, milk or both, should I layer the potatoes in the dish cooked or raw, and what about eggs and butter? Some cooks add them, but gosh, it's so rich already. The more recipes I researched, the more confused I became, so I gathered together as many varieties of potato as I could find, an assortment of milks, creams and flavourings, and headed to the kitchen.

The potatoes – which type?

Though many recipes I looked at didn't specify a variety, I wanted to see how the different ones reacted. My quest for the perfect potato began with the familiar King Edward. Six potato varieties later, of both the floury and waxy kind, I couldn't believe how each one completely altered the character of the dish. King Edward disappointed; for some reason the slices were a little tough on top. Charlotte gave slices that were too small, Marfona and Nicola didn't absorb the liquid that well and Estima was lacking in flavour. When the slices of Desirée potatoes were left out for too long, they mysteriously turned pale pink, but miraculously lost the tinge during cooking. Even so, I was won over by the Desirée. I loved the flavour and it behaved in just the way I wanted, keeping the layers beautifully separate while absorbing just the right amount of liquid during baking to leave a light, creamy sauce.

Slicing and layering

The width of the potato slices was going to be fairly crucial, both for the amount of liquid they absorbed and how well they cooked. I was drawn to the food processor for speed or the mandolin for its ease, but when it came to a more individual look, I opted for the traditional hand-slicing method. A knife also gave me more control for slicing the potatoes to the preferred thickness of 3mm/⅛in. Layering the potato in the dish raw appealed because it was less of a fuss, though I did try cooking them in the milk and cream before layering, which had been recommended as a way of reducing the starchiness. As well as complicating the method, the potatoes absorbed all the creaminess, so they were more like mash. I tried soaking the raw sliced potatoes in

water to lose some of the starch, but preferred them simply sliced and patted dry, as the starch proved useful for thickening the creamy milk. My attention now turned to the flavourings.

Refining the flavours

Classically, gratin Dauphinois is a very simple affair, the only constants I found being potatoes, cream and/or milk, a knob or a mound of butter (depending on the cook), with possibly a hint of garlic. Other recipes I browsed through added a wide range of herbs, crème fraîche as well as cream or milk, eggs, lemon juice, onion, nutmeg, Parmesan, Cheddar or Gruyère cheese. I wanted to give a subtle, pure savouriness without overcomplicating the dish, and lighten it rather than enrich it. After various attempts of adding chopped onion and herbs (too distracting in the layers) or crème fraîche (too solid), putting cheese and butter between the potatoes (far too greasy and rich) and rubbing garlic around the dish (a bit of a fiddle), I decided to add flavour by infusing the liquid (a blend of milk and cream gave a light creaminess) with my chosen flavourings, then straining them off to eliminate all the bits. This gave a purity of flavour and kept the potato as the hero of the dish.

1 You can use a mandolin to slice the potatoes.

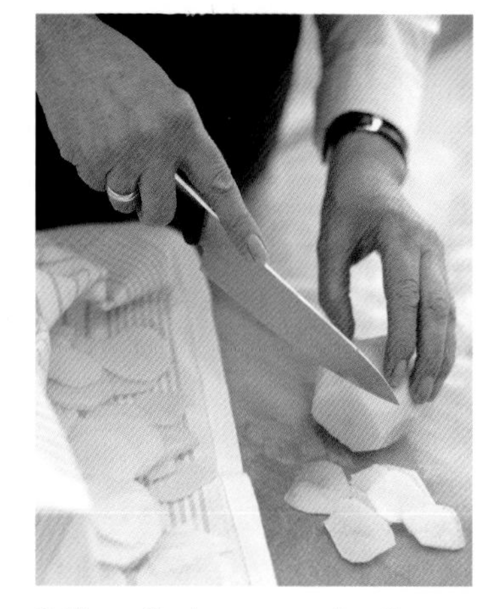

2 Alternatively you can slice them with a knife for better thickness control.

3 Strain the infused milk into a jug, sprinkle in the nutmeg and keep it all warm.

A discovery that made the dish

Heating the cream and milk to infuse it not only flavoured it more efficiently, but also speeded up the cooking process; it took much longer to cook from cold. A little Parmesan sprinkled over the final layer gave it a definite edge and, to reflect one of the flavours in the finished dish, I added a little scattering of fresh thyme leaves just before serving. The conclusion was more complicated to reach than anticipated, but the dish was simple and light yet creamy – just what I was after.

The recipe

Serves 6

Ready in just under 1½ hours

Easy

What you need

knob of butter
1kg/2lb 4oz Desirée potatoes
300ml/½ pint full-fat milk
284ml carton double cream
1 garlic clove, peeled and halved
2 sprigs of fresh thyme, plus extra for sprinkling
1 shallot, roughly chopped
pinch of freshly grated nutmeg
25g/1oz Parmesan, freshly grated

1 Heat the oven to 160°C/fan 140°C/Gas 4. Rub the butter all over the surface of a gratin dish, about 18 x 28cm/7 x 11in. Peel and slice the potatoes to a width of 3mm/⅛in. Lay the slices on a clean tea towel and pat dry. Keep them covered with the tea towel while you prepare the rest of the ingredients.

2 Pour the milk and cream into a saucepan. Add the garlic, thyme and shallot. Slowly heat the milk and, just as it is about to reach boiling point and you see bubbles appearing around the edge of the pan, remove it from the heat. Strain the liquid into a large jug, sprinkle in the nutmeg and keep it all warm.

3 Layer half the potato slices in the dish, slightly overlapping the slices and sprinkling with a little salt and freshly ground pepper between each layer. You don't have to be too neat with the lower layers, but keep some of your best slices for later, so the top looks good.

4 Pour half the hot milk and cream over the potatoes, then finish off layering the rest of the potatoes (arranging them a bit more carefully this time). Pour over the rest of the hot milk and cream. Scatter the Parmesan over the top and bake for about 1 hour, until golden and tender. Leave the dish to stand for about 5 minutes, then serve sprinkled with a few fresh thyme leaves.

Hot Chocolate Sauce

I knew I wouldn't have a problem finding tasters for this recipe, but I might have problems with the recipe if I got the chocolate wrong. I found recipes using semi-sweet or bitter, chocolate buttons, milk chocolate, even cocoa powder. For some expert advice I contacted self-confessed chocolate evangelist, Sara Jayne-Stanes, chairman of the Academy of Chocolate. 'You could use cocoa powder, but it won't have the smoothness,' Sara told me. 'Use the best chocolate there is,' she advised. 'If you use a really good one you will get liquid silk. If you use inferior chocolate you get inferior sauce. The best type is where the chocolate is allowed to speak for itself but not dominate.'

Getting a taste for it

When choosing chocolate my motto has always been: if you like the taste of it out of its wrapper, you will like it when it's cooked. Sara elaborated, 'if you eat chocolate and feel a frown, it's a bad one. You want to feel an immediate rapport with what's in your mouth, a combination of great pleasure, softness and intensity. Tasting chocolate is like tasting a fine wine. If it's cheap it will probably have a rough flavour.' You can check a chocolate's quality by looking on the wrapper, and the first thing Sara recommends finding out is the cocoa content. 'Around 70 per cent is a benchmark', she said, 'but 60 per cent can be good too – it depends on the quality and variety of the bean – you get what you pay for'. She also told me to look for natural ingredients, 'take vanilla, you don't want vanilla flavouring, it's pernicious.'

Melting begins

I wasn't even close to achieving the 'liquid silk' Sara spoke of, when the chocolate started to cause problems. Diverted by something else, I had allowed it to overcook and seize while being melted. I resolved this by being more attentive next time. I then read in Anne Willan's *How to Cook Absolutely Everything* (Quadrille Publishing): 'A reliable recipe for chocolate sauce will always call for enough liquid to melt the chocolate without danger of seizing.' This made me think – why was I melting the chocolate separately? Why not warm the liquid then let the chocolate melt in that, making it a one-pan sauce? This was foolproof.

Chocolate heaven

For liquid, I experimented with lots of cream. I got lots of sauce, but a diluted chocolate flavour. My favourite, for smooth consistency and just the right degree of richness, was a combination of mostly milk with a little double cream. I experimented with different chocolates. Cheaper ones infected the sauce with their sweetness. I got the complex, lingering chocolate flavour that Sara had said was vital, from a good-quality 70 per cent dark chocolate, but for a sauce, the tasters found it a bit too bitter. To balance the sweetness, I tried golden as well as corn syrup, thinking either would also add to the glossiness. They did, but the sauces looked plasticky and the syrupy sweetness overpowered. Instead, a balanced combination of sugar and butter didn't adulterate the chocolate taste and were less intrusive, and a pinch of coffee gave a surprising mellowness. As I poured the winning sauce from the spoon, it flowed like a glossy sheet of silk. Its taste was pure chocolate, neither too bitter nor domineering, but did I find enough tasters to agree with me? No problem.

The recipe

Makes about 250ml/9fl oz (enough for 4 servings), easily doubled

Ready in about 10 minutes

Easy

What you need

- 100g bar of best-quality bitter dark chocolate, 70 per cent cocoa solids (Green & Black's is good)
- 5 tbsp full-fat milk
- 2 tbsp double cream
- 25g/1oz golden caster sugar
- 25g/1oz butter, room temperature, diced
- ½ tsp instant coffee granules

Can be frozen

Make it boozy
Add 2–3 teaspoons of Amaretto to the milk.

1. Chop the chocolate fairly finely. Put the milk, cream, sugar, butter and coffee into a small pan. Bring to a boil, stirring with a wooden spoon until the sugar has dissolved and the butter melted. As soon as it comes to the boil, take the pan off the heat.
2. Stir in the chocolate, and keep stirring well until it has all melted and you have a smooth, silky sauce. Pour it into a bowl and leave to cool slightly. Serve while still warm. Use to pour generously over tarts, cream-filled meringues, vanilla ice cream and crêpes.

Storage tip
Keeps in the fridge for a couple of weeks (or can be frozen then thawed). Before serving, warm through in a bowl over a pan of gently simmering water, or in the microwave.

6

SIMPLY THE BEST BAKES AND CAKES

Scones

I thought I knew how to make scones – I've certainly made them enough times – but, as I have found before in my quest for the ultimate version of a dish, once I start delving into what appears to be a straightforward recipe, the possibilities become seemingly endless and more confusing. I began by whipping up the recipe I have had in my head for years (no need to look it up, even) using regular self-raising flour, milk, butter and sugar. What struck me now was how murky and lifeless the dough was. I immediately felt the culprit was the flour. Is it my imagination, or has flour changed over the years?

Ask the experts

Disheartened by my first batch, I called Darina Allen, who runs the Ballymaloe Cookery School in Ireland. 'Don't rub the flour and butter in too much,' she said, 'do it so it's in flakes, as it makes the dough a lot lighter. Also, you need to get the thickness of the dough just right. If it's too thick, the scones will topple over. If you roll them out too flat, the proportion of top crust to centre crumb will be wrong.'

Which type of flour?

I bought several bags of both plain and self-raising organic flour and went back to the kitchen to investigate the flour issue. I couldn't get over the difference organic flour made. The dough was more positive and purer – I would definitely stick with this. I always use just self-raising flour, but wanted to experiment with raising agents, so made up Darina's recipe, which called for plain flour with baking powder. I was impressed, even though some of the scones toppled over like miniature versions of the Leaning Tower of Pisa. I then realised that in my eagerness, I had mistakenly used self-raising flour with the baking powder! Quite a few recipes actually call for this combination, so I decided this was the way to go. I next turned to the overall flavour. It had to be butter and, with 225g/8oz of flour, 25g/1oz of sugar, it gave the best balance without being too sweet. Mid-experiment, I phoned Marguerite Patten, who must have made thousands of batches of wonderful scones in her time. 'If you get everything right, the scones will rise like a bird. I use self-raising flour, nothing added,' she said with conviction. 'Many go overboard with bicarbonate of soda and baking powder, but I loathe the taste of excess raising agent.' So I thought again about adding baking powder to the self-raising flour. 'On paper, scones look ridiculously easy,' confided Marguerite, 'but a lot of good cooks don't make good scones. Often they don't like to handle a moist dough.

I reckon to get slightly sticky when making scones.' I glanced down at my hands with bits of sticky dough clinging to them, and to the phone ... at least I was doing something right.

1 Rub the mixture to a reasonably fine-crumbed, slightly flaky texture and lift to aerate as you go.

How to make them rise

Feeling inspired, I lined up more bowls and mixed up doughs by the dozen. I began to fine-tune techniques, and found patting the dough rather than rolling it kept the whole thing lighter, something Scottish food writer Sue Lawrence had advised when I called her. 'The most important thing is to have an incredibly light touch,' she said. Scones don't rise as much as you think, and I found it best to give them a fighting chance by having the dough at least 2cm/¾in (but no more than 2.5cm/1in) thick before cutting them out. As to the cutter, it's an aesthetic choice whether you use the plain or the fluted sort. I opted for the friendly look the fluted one gave; the plain had a more commercial appearance.

2 Dip the cutter into flour to stop the dough sticking to it.

Getting the liquid right

Early on I found that full-fat milk made a lighter scone and egg wasn't necessary, but many other liquid choices were presenting themselves. Marguerite Patten said she used to make beautiful scones with soured milk, but she wouldn't do that now, as today's milk goes off before it sours. Remembering my mother making feather-light scones this way, I was eager to try food writer Moyra Fraser's take on this. 'I sour my own fresh milk with a squeeze of lemon juice, then leave it for half an hour,' she advised. I tried this, watched the milk magically turn almost yogurty, and thought I had the winner. The scone was proud and tall, and that faint hint of acidity and the chemical reaction it had unleashed really helped the flavour and lightness.

3 Aim for a thickness of 2–2.5cm/¾–1in.

And the winner is...

I had forgotten to try commercially made buttermilk, its acidic attributes being renowned in baking, so I threw caution to the wind and made a batch with self-raising flour (without extra baking powder), buttermilk mixed with a little milk to slacken it, and the fine-tuned measurements of butter, sugar and salt. I thrust the scones into a 220°C oven (the burst of heat this high temperature gave produced a slightly crisp edge to the scone with a lovely fluffy inside) and 10 minutes later, out came the real winners. They were all tall, straight and light and full of character. So if anyone asks you where you got this recipe from, you can say that it was the combined effort of myself, Marguerite Patten, Moyra Fraser, Sue Lawrence and Darina Allen.

The recipe

Makes 5–6 (easily doubled)

Ready in 25–35 minutes

Easy

What you need

225g/8oz self-raising flour, preferably organic
¼ tsp salt
50g/2oz slightly salted butter, chilled, cut into small pieces
25g/1oz golden caster sugar
125m/4fl oz buttermilk
4 tbsp full-fat milk
a little extra flour for dusting
strawberry jam and clotted cream, to serve

Can be frozen

Which glaze?
From top: a light sifting of flour (my favourite), beaten egg (nice and glossy), egg yolk (a bit garish) or buttermilk (too streaky).

1 Heat the oven to 220°C/fan 200°C/Gas 7 and lightly butter a baking sheet (unless you're using a non-stick sheet). Tip the flour into a mixing bowl with the salt. Add the butter, then rub together with your fingers to make a reasonably fine-crumbed mixture, lifting to aerate the mixture as you go. Try not to over-rub, as the mixture will be lighter if it's a little bit flaky. Now stir in the sugar.

2 Measure the buttermilk, then mix in the milk to slacken it. Make a bit of a well in the middle of the flour mixture with a round-bladed knife, then pour in most of this buttermilk mixture, holding a little bit back in case it's not needed. Using the knife, gently work the mixture together until it forms a soft, almost sticky, dough. Work in any loose dry bits of mixture with the rest of the buttermilk. Don't overwork at this point or you will toughen the dough.

3 Lift the ball of soft dough out of the bowl and put it onto a very lightly floured surface. Knead the mixture just 3–4 times to get rid of the cracks. Pat the dough gently with your hands to a thickness of no less than 2cm/¾in and no more than 2.5cm/1in. Dip a 5.5cm/2¼in round fluted cutter into a bowl of flour (this helps to stop the dough sticking to it), then cut out the scones by pushing down quickly and firmly on the cutter with the palm of your hand (don't twist it). You will hear the dough give a big sigh as the cutter goes in. Gather the trimmings lightly then pat and cut out a couple more scones.

4 Place on the baking sheet and sift over a light dusting of flour or glaze if you wish. Bake for 10–12 minutes until risen and golden. Cool on a wire rack, uncovered if you prefer crisp tops, or covered loosely with a cloth for soft ones.

5 Serve with strawberry jam and a generous mound of clotted cream (the Cornish put cream first, then jam, Devonians the other way round). Eat them as fresh as you can.

Blueberry Muffins

What fascinates me most about muffins is their size. To qualify for the name, they should be high-rise like their American counterparts, not resemble little buns. I didn't want them to be as enormous as those you buy in coffee shops, but I would work on getting them as big as I could, without letting their size take precedence over their texture and flavour.

Sizing things up

I knew how important a deep muffin tin was for the characteristic shape. My first decision was whether to line it with deep paper-cases or not. Though the cases made it extremely easy to remove the muffins, I found that when I peeled them off, a lot of the muffin stuck and was left behind. As long as I greased the holes in the tin generously and evenly, the muffins slipped out easily. They were also bigger. How much I filled the tins had an effect too. Half-filled, they came out looking too mean. I then tried overfilling them and although at first they just spilled over, I knew that once I had the balance of ingredients right, this would provide the high-rise effect.

Investigations continue

I had a choice of two mixing techniques: the traditional creaming of fat and sugar, or a much simpler way of mixing the dry ingredients into the wet. Being more familiar with the creaming method, which allows lots of air to be beaten in, I thought this would give a lighter muffin. I was wrong. Not only was the simpler method quicker, the muffins were lighter and less cakey. However, it required a much lighter touch than the creaming method. If the batter was over-mixed the muffins were tough. A lot of muffin recipes use oil as their fat, but butter was giving me better texture and flavour, and buttermilk was adding to the moistness and lightness. Plain flour plus baking powder gave the extra lift and stability I was after and, after experimenting with varying amounts of blueberries, I managed to pack in as many as I could, while still having enough batter mix to support them. In fact the muffins became so fruity, the berries were bursting with juiciness on the tops as they baked.

Dazzling tops

Now I just needed the tops to shine. Despite the bursting berries, they looked dull. I tried a sprinkling of sugar, but that wasn't dazzling enough. I then remembered a sugar glaze I make up to give hot cross buns their sheen. I had used lime zest in the batter, so I squeezed the juice, stirred in some sugar, and as the muffins emerged hot from the oven, brushed this over their mushrooming tops. Suddenly they were glamorous – there was no mistaking these majestic muffins for small buns.

The recipe

Makes 12 muffins

Ready in 40 minutes

Easy

What you need

85g/3oz butter, plus extra for buttering the tin
400g/14oz plain flour, preferably organic
1 tbsp baking powder
¼ tsp salt
175g/6oz golden caster sugar, plus 2 tbsp
1 lime
2 eggs
284ml carton buttermilk
2 x 150g cartons fresh blueberries

Can be frozen

1 Heat the oven to 200°C/fan 180°C/Gas 6. Melt the butter and leave it to cool slightly. Butter a 12-hole muffin tin. There's no need for paper-cases, but you could line each hole with a couple of crossed strips of baking parchment if you want, so they come just above the tops of the holes for easy removal. Sift the flour, baking powder and salt into a large bowl and stir in the 175g/6oz caster sugar. Finely grate the zest from the lime into the bowl.

2 Beat the eggs in another bowl, then stir in the buttermilk and cooled butter. Make a dip in the middle of the dry ingredients and pour in the buttermilk mixture. Gently stir with a big metal spoon for a few times only, until everything is only just combined. The mixture looks quite stiff, but feels light and spongy. If you over-mix now the muffins will be tough. Tip the blueberries in and stir a few more times to mix them in, again keeping a light touch and being careful not to over-mix.

3 Spoon the mixture into the tins so they are very full. Bake for about 25 minutes until the muffins have risen and are golden on top. Some of the blueberries may burst, but it will just make the muffins all the more juicy. While the muffins are baking, squeeze the juice from the lime and mix with the 2 tablespoons of sugar. This is the sugar glaze for the tops.

4 When the muffins are done, brush the tops with the sugar glaze then carefully loosen the sides with a round-bladed knife. Leave them to cool in the tin for about 5 minutes before lifting them out onto a wire rack to cool (they are a bit delicate to turn out while hot). Best eaten within two days.

Chocolate Chunk Cookies

This recipe was going to be called the ultimate chocolate 'chip' cookie, after one of America's best-loved cookies, which according to *The Fannie Farmer Cookbook* (Alfred A. Knopf) were created by a Massachusetts housewife in 1929. When I spoke with Lori Longbotham, cookbook author and a former Food Editor of *Gourmet Magazine* in New York, she told me that the one everyone considers to be their yardstick is the famous Tollhouse cookie made by Néstle. 'In America, chocolate chip cookies are the first thing everyone makes as a kid,' Lori said, 'and because they follow the recipe on the back of the packet, that is their favourite.' I managed to get hold of the original recipe and quickly had a batch baking in the oven. They were good – sweet and crisp – but more like bought cookies and the little chips seemed lost. I decided to go for a more chocolatey experience, so out went the 'chips' to be replaced with 'chunks' – in name also. My craving was to be able to bite through a crisp outside into a brownie-like softness inside.

A fine balancing act

I experimented with different amounts of flour to sugar to butter to egg. Adjusting the amount of chocolate could come later; it was the fine balance of all these ingredients that would give me the texture I was after. I wanted the cookies to spread a little in the oven, but still keep a good shape, leaving room for that slender layer of brownie chewiness in the centre. When the ingredients were out of balance, the cookies either spread so much they were as flat as pancakes, or they didn't move at all and stayed in stiff, upright mountainous piles on the baking sheet. Getting the sugar right proved key. When I used all caster sugar, I just got sweet crispiness. I tried muscovado which gave a better flavour, but it was the blend of both that improved both texture and taste. The next thing to sort out was their size. I've seen these cookies as big as saucers but when Lori told me that oversized cookies were a '1980s thing', I went for quality over quantity to bring them into the 21st century.

Getting the chocolate right

Chunks of chocolate were definitely making the cookies more appealing, but I also favoured them over the chips as I could introduce a better quality of chocolate. I got rather carried away to begin with, to the point where there was more chocolate than cookie batter. I cut it back, as I also wanted to leave room for a few nuts. Although Lori warned me that some people consider it a real travesty to add nuts to this type of cookie, I really liked the combination, plus it added to their chunkiness. As the final batch lay cooling, I could see these cookies were definitely living up to their name.

The recipe

Makes 16–17 cookies

Ready in about 45–50 minutes (as cooking is done in several batches)

Easy

What you need

2 x 100g bars good-quality dark chocolate (at least 55 per cent cocoa solids, preferably 70 per cent)
1 tsp instant coffee granules
100g bar milk chocolate
115g/4oz light muscovado sugar
25g/1oz golden caster sugar
115g/4oz butter, at room temperature
1 egg
½ tsp vanilla extract
115g/4oz plain flour
½ tsp bicarbonate of soda
100g packet pecans, broken into biggish chunks

Can be frozen
Or will keep in an airtight tin for up to 2–3 days

1 Heat the oven to 180°C/fan 160°C/Gas 4. Get all the ingredients weighed out. Break 85g/3oz of the dark chocolate into a large heatproof bowl, sprinkle in the coffee and melt the chocolate (over a pan of gently simmering water, or in the microwave on Medium for about 1½ minutes). Stir. Chop or break the milk chocolate and the rest of the dark chocolate into big chunks.
2 Tip both the sugars, the butter (cut into small pieces), the whole egg and the vanilla into the melted chocolate and beat well with a wooden spoon to a dark, silky smooth batter. Mix the flour and bicarbonate of soda. Stir this into the chocolate batter just to combine, then stir in most of the nuts and the chocolate chunks, keeping back a handful of each to put on top of the cookies later. The mixture is quite soft.
3 Drop a few heaped teaspoonfuls of the mixture onto a baking sheet, keeping each one well apart so they have room to spread. Lightly press 2–3 pieces of the reserved chocolate chunks and nuts into the top of each cookie.
4 You will need to bake the cookies in batches as there will only be room on the sheet for a few at a time. Bake for about 12 minutes until they are just starting to turn a darker brown around the edges. Leave the cookies to cool on the baking sheet for about 5 minutes, as they are quite fragile when they come out of the oven. Lift them onto a wire rack with a wide spatula so they can cool completely. Once they are cold they will be firm and crisp on the outside, softer in the centre.

Meringues

Rules are made to be bent, sometimes even broken. So when I read in my classic Cordon Bleu book that for Swiss meringues 'the proportion of sugar to egg white never varies, being 2oz caster sugar to each egg white,' I felt like a rebel with a cause. I was out to break the rules and see how far I could manipulate these two simple ingredients to my culinary ends. First, a quick look at the possibilities. There are three meringue types: Swiss (the ordinary type, egg whites whisked with caster sugar); Italian (made with sugar syrup, for a crisp, more powdery meringue) and meringue cuite (very stable, egg whites and icing sugar whisked over a gentle heat, to give a fine, chalky texture). I wanted to pursue the more well-used Swiss one. My goal was for a billowy, shapely meringue, colour off-white, and crisp outside with a soft melt-in-the-mouth centre. Above all, a meringue with taste, apart from just sugar.

Everyone does it differently

A brief chat with a few experts always gets me focused, so I rang Mary Berry, queen of baking. Having read in various books how the eggs must come from the fridge, be whisked in a copper bowl, that meringues should be made only with white sugar, should have no colour after baking, I was heartened by Mary's remarks. 'I couldn't give a stuff whether the eggs come from the fridge or are at room temperature, and whether you use a copper bowl or not doesn't matter, as long as it's clean. Also, I don't like white meringues, I prefer them to look creamy.' She also wasn't averse to substituting a bit of brown sugar for white – a fellow rebel indeed. Mary adds the sugar a spoonful at a time, which she claims prevents any weeping. This I duly noted. Baker Dan Lepard gave me quite different advice. His proportion of caster sugar to egg whites was much greater, the oven temperature higher, and his method of warming raw egg whites with all the sugar before beating them together seemed more unconventional. I even went to see Ian Thomason, senior sous chef at the Savoy, London. In the hotel's kitchen, out came the KitchenAid food mixer, and for their interpretation of Swiss meringue, the caster sugar was added all at once to the barely beaten whites to create a shiny foam that was great for piping, as Ian demonstrated. It's how they have always done it, and it works for them.

Testing begins

I began my testing with the classic recipe in order to work out exactly which rules I wanted to bend. I whisked the egg whites first until they were like fluffy clouds, as Mary Berry had suggested. Caster sugar

(50g/2oz per egg white) was whisked in very gradually, then one half of the mixture was baked at fan 110°C, the other in a conventional oven at 130°C. The result? Absolutely nothing wrong with them. This was too easy. Interestingly, though, the batch in the fan oven came out white, and the one in the conventional oven was pale coffee-coloured. As a complete contrast, I turned to Dan Lepard's recipe. He suggested heating the whites and sugar until the sugar dissolved and the whites felt warm. Knowing how quickly eggs can overheat and what havoc it can cause, I nervously began, but all was fine, and soon I was whisking the contents of the pan (now in a bowl, off the heat) to a thick glossy mass. The resulting meringues were shiny, and crisp all through, with quite a bit of cracking and weeping going on. Nice, but not quite what I was after.

1 Beat the egg whites until the mixture stands up in stiff peaks.

Fantastic – almost caramelly

I then came across a recipe by French chef Alain Ducasse. His method was rather vague, but what intrigued me was the fact that he used half caster sugar and half icing sugar, in much greater proportions to the egg white than the classic recipe advises. Also, he beat in the caster, then folded in the icing sugar. I got out the whisk again and ended up with meringues that had a lovely crust (albeit a bit thick and craggy) and a wonderful marshmallowy inside. The taste was fantastic, almost caramelly – definitely what I was after. I deduced this was coming from the combination of sugars. Now all I needed to do was to clone the best characteristics from all the recipes I had tried so far, in order to create the ultimate.

2 Before adding the icing sugar, the mixture should be thick and glossy.

Tweaking the recipe and method

To this end I began whisking in earnest. Adding icing sugar definitely improved the crust and taste, I just needed to work on the amount. (I tried organic, unrefined sugar, but unfortunately the result did not look as good.) After much experimentation I combined Mary Berry's technique of adding the caster sugar slowly and Alain Ducasse's of folding in the icing sugar, which worked beautifully. I found underwhisking gave poor volume, while overwhisking caused cracking; it was vital to get it just right at each stage. Next, to satisfy my curiosity, cornflour was added to see whether it affected the texture, as in a pavlova, but the rather collapsed look it gave wasn't right. Then there was the choice of which implement to use for the whisking. Dan Lepard remembered his grandmother using two forks, but I opted for the electric hand-whisk. I preferred this over the KitchenAid as I could manipulate the beaters round the bowl better in order to aerate the mixture, while they did all the hard work. I also tried a balloon whisk but it did not increase volume or lightness, only the muscles of my arm.

3 Use dessertspoons to create oval shapes with the mixture.

Final decision – how to cook

Now happy with the recipe (using half caster, half icing) and the method, I had one big decision left to make: how best to cook the meringues. I found that when the oven was kept on all the time, a lower temperature gave the marshmallow interior I was after (timing was important here too; left in too long, its cloud-like texture became thin and chewy), and the conventional oven gave a crisper crust and preferred colour and flavour. Then it suddenly came to me to increase the fan temperature and cook them a bit longer, and this gave a more similar result to the conventional oven. I may not have been quite the rebel I had hoped to be but, gosh, my hybrid meringues were by now everything I had hoped for.

The recipe

Makes 16

Ready in 1 hour 35 mins – just over 2 hours (depending on the oven)

Fairly easy

What you need

4 egg whites, preferably organic, at room temperature
115g/4oz caster sugar
115g/4oz icing sugar
softly whipped double cream, to fill

Can be frozen (unfilled)

1 Heat the oven to 110°C/fan 100°C/Gas ¼. Line 2 baking sheets with Bake-O-Glide non-stick liner or parchment paper (meringue can stick on greaseproof paper and foil).

2 Tip the egg whites into a large clean mixing bowl (not plastic). Beat them on medium speed with an electric hand-whisk until the mixture resembles a fluffy cloud and stands up in stiff peaks when the blades are lifted.

3 Now turn the speed up and start to add the caster sugar, a dessertspoonful at a time. Continue beating for 3–4 seconds between each addition. It's important to add the sugar slowly at this stage as it helps prevent the meringue from weeping later. However, don't over-beat. When ready, the mixture should be thick and glossy.

4 Sift a third of the icing sugar over the mixture, then gently fold it in with a big metal spoon or rubber spatula. Continue to sift and fold in the icing sugar a third at a time. Again, don't over-mix. The mixture should now look smooth and billowy, almost like a snow drift.

5 Scoop up a heaped dessertspoonful of the mixture. Using another dessertspoon, ease it onto the baking sheet to make an oval shape (or just drop them in rough rounds, if you prefer). Bake for 1½–1¾ hours in a fan oven, 1¼ hours in a conventional or gas oven, until the meringues sound crisp when tapped underneath and are a pale coffee colour. Leave to cool on the trays or a wire rack. (The meringues will now keep in an airtight tin for up to 2 weeks, or frozen for a month.) Serve two meringues sandwiched together with a generous dollop of softly whipped double cream.

Flapjacks

I've often had trouble with flapjacks. They've either been too sweet, greasy, crumbly or sticky. Not surprising considering the ingredients that are used. However, when the sugar, butter, oats and syrup come together in a balanced way, these bars are one of the most irresistibly addictive bakes you can make. I found that not everyone's idea of the ultimate flapjack was the same. Some favoured crisp and crunchy, others thick and chewy, or something in between. To satisfy as many tastes as possible, I opted to create a texture that was crisp on the outside, soft and chewy in the centre – a flapjack that wouldn't fall apart, or make your teeth stick together.

Balancing sweetness and stickiness

Making flapjacks is child's play – you just melt and stir – but things can easily go wrong. Take the sugar. Each type gives a different result. After experimenting with caster and brown sugars, I preferred unrefined light muscovado as it added a subtle sweetness and taste too. However, I wasn't getting the outer crunch I wanted. Butter over margarine gave me flavour and golden syrup helped to stick everything together, but how much syrup to use? Some recipes I looked at suggested no more than a tablespoonful, while others called for up to 140g/5oz. Balancing sweetness and stickiness was important, so I called Mary Berry for her opinion. What intrigued me about her recipe was that she used demerara sugar, and lots of it. 'It gives a nice caramelly mixture,' she told me. I wondered how it would melt and blend with the oats, so whipped up a batch. Towards the end of cooking the sugar started to caramelise on the surface. This gave me my crispy top, but I had lost some of the flavour. So I decided to keep enough demerara for crispness, with syrup to bind, and reintroduce light muscovado for flavour.

A happy accident

To overcome excessive sweetness, greasiness and fragility, I then played around with the proportions of butter, sugars, syrup and oats. The absorbency of the oats was key. I soon recognised just how moist the raw mix needed to be, and once I had fine-tuned this I hurriedly mixed up one final test in metric. I couldn't understand why the mix was wetter than the imperial, then looking through the oven door as it baked I noticed the mixture bubbling up with juiciness. Sounds delicious, but something was wrong. As I cut them they completely fell apart, and a sweet butteriness oozed out. Glancing at the pack of oats I had used, the label read 'jumbo oats'. In my haste I had grabbed the wrong packet. This accident confirmed what Mary Berry had advised. 'It's important to say which oats you use, as it makes a difference. I use rolled (porridge) oats as whole or jumbo absorb a different amount.' Another batch was quickly mixed and as I contentedly chewed my way through it, I knew my troubles with flapjacks were finally over.

The recipe

Cuts into 12 bars

Ready in 35–40 minutes, plus cooling

Easy

What you need
225g/8oz slightly salted butter, cut into pieces
140g/5oz demerara sugar
50g/2oz light muscovado sugar
3 level tbsp golden syrup
325g/11oz rolled porridge oats (not jumbo)

Can be frozen
Or will keep in an airtight tin for up to a week

Extra-crunchy topping
Before baking, scatter the top fairly liberally with sunflower seeds or a mix of sunflower, pumpkin seeds and pine nuts.

1 Heat the oven to 180°C/fan 160°C/Gas 4. Line the base of a 28 x 18cm/11 x 7in shallow baking tin with baking or greaseproof paper. (If you dab a bit of butter in each corner of the tin first it will hold the paper down.) Put the butter, both the sugars and the golden syrup in a medium pan. Stir over a low heat until the butter has melted and the sugar is starting to dissolve (it doesn't need to completely dissolve, but everything should be combined).
2 Take the pan off the heat and stir in the oats until you have a soft, sticky mixture. Tip this into the tin and spread it out, gently pressing it down so it is even. You don't need to completely smooth the top, in fact it's more interesting with a bit of rough texture.
3 Bake for 20–25 minutes until golden brown. Carefully loosen the sides with a round-bladed knife (otherwise they will stick as they cool), then, as the mixture is very soft, leave it to cool in the tin for a couple of minutes. It should feel crisp on top when you tap it, and will be softer inside. Mark into 12 bars while still warm and leave to cool in the tin completely. If you take the flapjacks out while still warm, they are likely to break up. Tip the flapjacks out onto a board, turn them over and cut through the marks into bars.

Banana Nut Bread

From now on I'm always going to leave a few bananas to blacken in the fruit bowl, on the off-chance that I get the urge to make banana bread. Though many recipes call for ripe bananas, it's a vague term, and I'm usually too impatient so use what I have, then wonder why the flavour and texture varies so much. After all the testing, I'm now sure that success is all down to the banana, and that ripeness means blackness.

In search of something different

Unusually, I found little difference with the many recipes I looked at. Even amounts of ingredients didn't vary much, so I began to wonder what new element I could bring to this favourite quick-bread. I did want to move away from the heaviness often described as a characteristic, and perhaps an iced topping would cheer it up? Being a popular bake in North America, many recipes called for plain flour with the addition of baking power or bicarbonate of soda, or both (self-raising flour being less available there). To make the recipe more practical, I made one up with self-raising flour to avoid the use of raising agents. For something more extravagant, I mixed in macadamia nuts rather than the usual walnuts or pecans. However, I couldn't have been more disappointed – the cake was dense, heavy and lacking in flavour. What had caused it? I had used three large bananas, but would never have guessed it, and the macadamia nuts weren't offering much flavour either. Perhaps too much flour had gone in? Not enough sugar? Had I been too heavy-handed when mixing?

Unexpected discovery

I started again and decided to reject macadamia nuts in favour of pecans, which I toasted first to bring out their special flavour, and for subtle background flavouring, I would stir in a touch of lemon and vanilla. For lightness I would spoon in a little soured cream, reduce the flour slightly and reintroduce plain plus raising agents. Eager to start mixing, I went to the fruit bowl for bananas. The only ones left had turned completely black. Should I throw them out or mix them in? Recalling how these are favoured by Caribbean cooks for their intense sweetness and flavour, I began peeling. What struck me too, as I compared their weight with the less ripe ones I had been using, was how much lighter they were, and the fork mashed through them effortlessly.

A winner emerges

I had high hopes this time, and as the bread baked I could smell I was onto a winner as the bananas' sweetness mingled with the toasted aroma of the nuts. I realised that leaving the bananas to blacken had concentrated their flavour and sweetness, reduced the amount used, and when the bread emerged from the oven, all signs of heaviness had gone. With its light texture and well-defined flavour, the bread's simplicity was its strength; an icing would be mere frivolity.

The recipe

Cuts into 12 slices

Ready in about 1 hour 25 minutes, includes an hour or so in the oven

Easy

What you need

100g/4oz pecan nuts
about 3 extremely ripe medium bananas, the blacker the skins, the better
finely grated zest of ½ lemon
1 tsp vanilla extract
225g/8oz plain flour
1 tsp baking powder
½ tsp bicarbonate of soda
115g/4oz butter, room temperature
140g/5oz light muscovado sugar
2 eggs, beaten
4 tbsp soured cream

Can be frozen

Or will keep well wrapped for up to 4–5 days. It becomes more moist and the banana flavour more intense after a day or two. If you still have some left after 4 days it may be drier, but is good buttered.

1 Heat the oven to 180°C/fan 160°C/Gas 4. Butter a 20 x 13cm/8 x 5in loaf tin, and line the bottom with baking parchment. Tip the nuts onto a baking sheet and toast them in the oven for 10–12 minutes or until they look darker in colour. Let them cool slightly, keep 8–9 halves back and break the rest into rough pieces. Peel the bananas, break them in several pieces into a bowl, then mash them with a fork so the banana is as smooth as you can get it. (A few small lumps won't matter.) You should have about 225g/8oz mashed banana. (Too much banana can make the bread heavy.) Stir in the lemon zest and vanilla. Mix the flour with the baking powder and bicarbonate of soda.

2 Beat the butter and sugar in a large bowl for a couple of minutes with an electric hand-whisk, scraping the sides of the bowl down once or twice, until the mix looks paler in colour, and drops softly from the scraper. Whisk in the eggs a third at a time, beating well after each lot is added. Lightly stir in the mashed banana and the soured cream. The mixture will look very curdled, but it will be fine once the flour goes in. Gently fold the flour mix in with a large metal spoon, half at a time. It's best not to over-mix. Stir in about ¾ of the broken nuts.

3 Spoon the mixture into the tin and smooth the top. Scatter the saved halved pecans and the rest of the broken ones over the bread and bake for 1 hour, or until it is risen, feels firm and when a skewer pushed into the middle comes out without any raw mixture sticking to it. (If the nuts start to brown too much towards the end of cooking, lay a strip of foil loosely over the top.) If it's not quite cooked, return it to the oven for another 5 minutes and test again.

4 Leave the banana bread in the tin for 5 minutes to cool slightly, then loosen the sides with a round-bladed knife before turning it out onto a wire rack. Peel off the lining paper, and leave the bread to cool completely.

Chocolate Cake

When a friend mentioned she had spent all weekend searching in vain for a decent chocolate cake recipe she could make with her daughter, I took it as a challenge. The recipe my mother had always used involved replacing a spoonful of flour with a spoonful of cocoa powder. I loved it at the time, but that was as chocolatey as it got. Looking through British cookbooks, I found most chocolate cake recipes are still based on a traditional creamed cake with cocoa powder to flavour – chocolate by name, but nothing like it in taste.

Breaking with tradition

It was food writer Ruth Watson's comments that gave me the notion to break away from the constraints of a classic creamed cake. 'I favour a moist, soggy, sad cake,' she told me. Sounded odd, but I knew what she meant. She too had difficulty finding the recipe she was after. 'I can't tell you how many I've tried. All the ones that say they are the "ultimate" seem to miss it, using just cocoa powder. You might get flavour, but certainly not texture.'

Looking afar for help

I saw the direction I needed to go in. Having lived in North America, I knew Americans were more carefree in the way they made cakes. They were less bound by tradition and more decadent. I became determined to do, and add, whatever it took to create the gooiest, moistest, fudgiest, chocolatiest cake ever. Something like a brownie with layers. So, apologies now to anyone on a diet. This recipe will not be for you.

The simple method was a winner

Weighing, mixing and beating began in earnest. Cakes rose, fell, cracked and split as I varied proportions and methods. What soon became clear was, the simpler the method and the softer the mixture, the better the cake. As I narrowed my options, I was no longer carefully creaming, but melting butter with chocolate, and lots of it. Liquid was going in, as was buttermilk, which magically improved the texture and cut the sugary taste. A shot of coffee brought out the chocolate flavour, and longer, slower cooking helped keep the cake moist. I was still adding cocoa powder, but purely as a back-up to melted good-quality chocolate. As I poured this sea of dark silkiness into the cake tin, I just knew it was going to taste good. It was as far away from a chocolate Victoria sandwich as you could imagine, and required little skill.

Sugar is the key

When I had a recipe I was almost happy with, food writer Lulu Grimes showed me an Australian recipe she swore by. It had many similarities to mine, except the amount of sugar was higher, much higher. So, I tried adding more sugar and it certainly made a difference to the texture and, amazingly, was not oversweet. It also gave the slight brownie characteristic I was after, while still allowing me to slice the cake for layering. I tried using half muscovado and half caster, and preferred the slight fudginess the blend gave and how it balanced the flavours. After a few more tweaks – and inches on the hips – the recipe was done. A simple chocolate ganache icing gave it the sophistication it deserved and I sent the recipe to Ruth Watson for her approval. Her verdict? 'It's beautifully chocolatey, not too sweet, not too bitter, perfect as a dessert cake.'

1 Stir the cake mixture until you have a smooth, quite runny consistency.

2 Sandwich the cake layers with a little of the ganache then pour the rest over the cake.

3 Use a sawing motion when pushing the chocolate along the surface to make curls, then lift them off.

The recipe

Cuts into 14 slices

Ready in
about 2 hours, includes baking but not cooling time

Easy

Please follow either metric or imperial measures precisely

What you need
200g/8oz good-quality dark chocolate, about 60% cocoa solids
200g/8oz butter, cut into pieces
1 tbsp instant coffee granules
85g/3oz self-raising flour
85g/3oz plain flour
¼ tsp bicarbonate of soda
200g/7oz light muscovado sugar
200g/7oz golden caster sugar
25g/1oz cocoa powder
3 medium eggs
75ml/2½fl oz buttermilk (5 tbsp)
grated chocolate or curls, to decorate

For the ganache
200g/8oz good-quality dark chocolate, as above
284ml carton double cream (pouring type)
2 tbsp golden caster sugar

Can be frozen (without icing)

1 Butter a 20cm/8in round cake tin (7.5cm/3in deep) and line the base. Heat the oven to 160°C/fan 140°C/Gas 3. Break the chocolate in pieces into a medium, heavy-based pan. Tip in the butter, then mix the coffee granules into 125ml/4fl oz cold water and pour into the pan. Warm through over a low heat just until everything is melted (don't overheat), or melt in the microwave on Medium for about 5 minutes, stirring halfway through.
2 While the chocolate is melting, mix the two flours, bicarbonate of soda, sugars and cocoa in a big bowl, mixing with your hands to get rid of any lumps. Beat the eggs in a bowl and stir in the buttermilk.
3 Now pour the melted chocolate mixture and the egg mixture into the flour mixture, stirring just until everything is well blended and you have a smooth, quite runny consistency. Pour this into the tin and bake for 1 hour 25–1 hour 30 minutes. If you push a skewer into the centre it should come out clean and the top should feel firm (don't worry if it cracks a bit). Leave to cool in the tin (don't worry if it dips slightly), then turn it out onto a wire rack to cool completely.
4 When the cake is cold, cut it horizontally into three. Make the ganache: chop the chocolate into small pieces and tip into a bowl. Pour the cream into a pan, add the sugar, and heat until it is about to boil. Take off the heat and pour it over the chocolate. Stir until the chocolate has melted and the mixture is smooth.
5 Sandwich the layers together with just a little of the ganache. Pour the rest over the cake, letting it fall down the sides and smoothing to cover with a palette knife. Decorate with grated chocolate or a pile of chocolate curls. The cake keeps moist and gooey for 3–4 days.

How to make chocolate curls
This may take a little practice. Spread a thin layer of melted chocolate onto a flat surface, preferably marble, or use a chopping board. When the chocolate appears set (it should look matt and still be slightly soft), hold a firm, long-bladed knife at a 45 degree angle to the surface and, using a sawing motion, push the chocolate along the surface to make curls. Remove to set firmly. If the chocolate is on a board, you can speed up the chocolate's setting process by putting it in the fridge for a few minutes, but keep an eye on it so it doesn't get too hard, as it will then be impossible to curl.

Carrot Cake

In its heyday of the 1970s, it was the trendy North American cake to serve at weddings. It is still enjoyed as a fashionable café slice but the originality of carrot cake was its use of oil instead of butter, which has been both its strength and downfall. Its strength because oil provides the potential for an easy-mix, moist cake. Its downfall as too much oil is often added, leaving the cake as well as your hands as you eat it, extremely greasy. To update the cake, I would find ways to eliminate greasiness and make it light yet moist, then decide whether it really needed an icing.

Attending to the cake

Carrots give this cake moistness, but I found that if I grated in too many it was heavy; too few and it was dry. Then baker Tom Dolby of Tom's Cakes in Cambridgeshire told me his secret for achieving moistness and lack of greasiness. 'I make an orange purée by cooking and liquidizing oranges, sugar and water. Because you have the liquid of the orange pulp, you don't need as much oil,' he told me. I liked the idea, but not the extra work. I found recipes that included canned crushed pineapple. Perhaps this would have a similar effect? It just gave me sogginess. As a compromise, I soaked raisins in a little orange juice. With this extra liquid and plumped-up fruity flavour, and the correct amount of carrot, I then reduced the oil. All signs of greasiness disappeared, and I was left with lightness and moistness. Creating a stablized mix with the sugar, eggs and oil before adding the flour, and baking the cake in a low oven, also helped the light texture. To balance the flavours I had switched from light muscovado sugar to dark, stirred in toasted nuts and orange zest and confined the spice to cinnamon rather than the confusing mix that I had been using.

Tackling the icing

I was delighted with the cake and some tasters felt it was good enough to forgo an icing, but there is something about the traditional cream-cheese icing that has always troubled me and I wanted to get to the bottom of it. Why does it go runny when the icing sugar is added? I tried everything to keep it firm, also less sweet and rich. I chilled it, beat in lemon juice to set it, tried adding less sugar, more soft cheese, switched honey for icing sugar, mascarpone for soft cheese, even beat in white chocolate and nothing worked. Eight bowlfuls of icing later I came up with a solution inspired by something Tom Dolby had said. 'I make a butter-cream icing first and add the cream cheese to it. Somehow it helps stabilize it.' Miraculously it did. By completely changing the method, using less cream cheese and sugar, flavouring with orange zest and lemon juice, I had discovered an updated, fresher icing that perfectly partnered my updated cake.

The recipe

Cuts into 16 pieces

Ready in about 1½ hours

Easy

What you need
For the cake
85g/3oz brazil nuts
1 medium orange
115g/4oz raisins
225g/8oz self-raising flour
1 tsp bicarbonate of soda
1 rounded tsp ground cinnamon
175g/6oz dark muscovado sugar
175ml/6fl oz sunflower oil
3 eggs
280g/10oz finely grated carrot (2–3 carrots)

For the icing
50g/2oz icing sugar
50g/2oz butter, softened
100g/4oz full-fat soft cheese, room temperature
finely grated zest of 1 small orange
1 tsp lemon juice

Can be frozen ('Open-freeze' the iced cake by freezing it without wrapping until firm. Then wrap it and return it to the freezer. This way the icing doesn't get squashed.)
Or will keep for up to 5 days un-iced in an airtight tin, or in the fridge if iced

1 Heat the oven to 160°C/fan 140°C/Gas 3. Put the nuts on a small baking sheet and toast in the oven for about 15 minutes. Meanwhile, for the cake, finely grate the zest from the orange and set aside. Squeeze the juice from half the orange (you need 2 tablespoons) and pour it over the raisins in a bowl. Stir and leave to soak while you make the cake. Oil and line the base of a deep 20cm/8in square cake tin with baking parchment. Mix the flour, bicarbonate of soda and cinnamon. Chop the toasted nuts fairly finely.

2 Tip the sugar into a large mixing bowl, and rub it between your fingers to break up any lumps. Pour in the oil, then with an electric hand-mixer, beat them together on a low speed, until well mixed and you have broken down as many of the little lumps of sugar as you can (you'll find dark muscovado is a bit harder to mix than light). Add the eggs one at a time, beating well after each one is added. The mixture resembles runny toffee. Tip in the flour mix and gently stir it into the egg mixture with a large metal spoon. The mixture now looks like thick toffee.

3 Fold in the carrots, nuts, raisins (and any liquid) and reserved orange zest (the mixture is quite soft, like a thick batter), then pour it into the tin. Bake for 1 hour until risen, firm on top, or until a skewer comes out clean when inserted in the centre. If not done, return the cake to the oven for another 5–10 minutes and test again. Let the cake cool in the tin for 5 minutes, then turn it out onto a wire rack, peel off the lining paper and leave to go completely cold.

4 While the cake cools you can make the icing. Sift the icing sugar if lumpy. Beat the butter and icing sugar together until smooth (a wooden spoon is fine), then beat in the soft cheese, then the orange zest and lemon juice. Spread it over the cold cake, give it a swirl and serve cut into squares or slices. This cake is even better if left for a day or two before icing and eating.

7

THE FINAL WORD ON PUDDINGS

Crêpes Suzettes

Crêpes suzettes is a rather pretentious dessert – all that tossing and flambéeing – so it's hardly surprising that it has fallen from grace over the years. Even London's Savoy restaurant has taken it off its menu. Yet the more I read about it, the more I was reminded of its attributes. So, my challenge has been to strip away all the complications and give crêpes suzettes back its rightful place as a delightful dessert. Who was Suzette? Some say she was an actress, and one story goes that the chef Henri Charpentier invented the dish at the Café de Paris in Monte Carlo for the future Edward VII, Suzette being a young girl in the Prince's lunch party.

Making the batter

French crêpes are lighter, frillier and more dainty than British pancakes. To achieve this I made various batters: in a bowl with a wooden spoon and in a blender. The blender batter was super-quick, but the crêpes were rubbery. I made a version with whole eggs, one with a combination of one egg and one egg yolk, and a rich version with full-fat milk and cream. The first two batters were light with an ideal consistency of single cream, the third was much thicker. I consulted the proprietor of London's Mon Plaisir restaurant, M. Alain Lhermitte, who passed on his secret: adding a 'touch' of beer to the batter. When I tipped it in, little bubbles frothed, giving the batter just the liveliness I was after. I could now let it sit for several hours, or start cooking immediately. I did both and found little difference.

Finding the right pan

I have several types of pans but one stood out. It was strong, thick-based, with gently sloping sides and a well-used, yet cared-for, look. I tried others that were shinier, newer than the one I liked – the batter stuck to the non-stick pan – but seasoning the traditional cast-iron pan (by heating and wiping with oil and salt) worked like a dream. Its shape and shallow sides also made turning the crêpes far easier. Nothing was a match for it.

Cooking the crêpes

My first crêpe slid out crisp and pale. The pan was not hot enough, so the crêpes dried out, rather than browned; but too hot and they will burn. The best way to test is to splash a drop of water into the pan – if it splutters and evaporates, it is ready. As I worked my way through the various batters, it reminded me how the cooking of crêpes becomes

instinctive: getting the right temperature of the pan and the right amount of batter, and when and how to turn the crêpes. Measuring 2½ tablespoons of batter into a jug and pouring it into the pan made it easier to swirl. Then I just poured in an unmeasured amount, swirled the pan around, tipped out the excess, trimmed the edge and had crêpes that required less skill, although they were slightly thicker.

The verdict

The crêpes made with full-fat milk and cream were heavy and looked like chamois leather. The ones made with two whole eggs plus the splash of beer were my favourites – thin, light and with the appearance of a delicate French lace doily. All they needed now was to be bathed in a tasty sauce.

Creating the sauce

Every recipe I read was different. I could use tangerines rather than oranges, Cointreau or curaçao instead of the usual Grand Marnier. I could scent the sugar with citrus peel, flambé or not. I decided to keep it simple but well flavoured. As most chefs I talked to preferred Grand Marnier because of its colour, I chose that, along with some cognac, plus a delicate balance of lemon and orange zests and juice; I decided to caramelise the sugar to concentrate the flavour and colour. I also tried flambéeing, but it added nothing by way of flavour, only drama.

Make-ahead tip
If making crêpes a day ahead: wrap and keep in the fridge. Warm through in the sauce. To reheat them to serve just with lemon or syrup, put on an ovenproof plate, cover with foil and warm in a 180°C/ fan 160°C/Gas 4 oven for 10–15 minutes.

1 Less skill is required if you swirl the batter in the pan then pour off the excess into a jug.

2 Or, for thinner crèpes, pour a measured amount of batter into the pan then move it around so the mixture covers the bottom.

3 For the sauce, pour the orange juice into the caramelised sugar before adding the zests.

Marrying crêpes and sauce

To bring the two together, I swished the crêpes one at a time in the sauce so that they were well coated. I then folded them in four as you would a lady's handkerchief, as suggested by Henri Charpentier. I was pleased with them and I hope Suzette would have been, too.

The recipe

Serves 6
(16–17 dainty crêpes, 2–3 per person)

Ready in 40–45 minutes

Fairly easy

What you need

For the crêpe batter

100g/4oz plain flour
1 tbsp golden caster sugar
2 eggs
1 tbsp sunflower oil
300ml/½ pint semi-skimmed milk
splash of beer, about 2 tbsp (optional)

For the sauce

100g/4oz butter
100g/4oz golden caster sugar
150ml/¼ pint freshly-squeezed orange juice (about 2 large oranges)
2 tsp finely grated orange zest
1 tsp finely grated lemon zest
3 tbsp Grand Marnier
2 tbsp cognac

Can be frozen (crêpes only)

1 To make the crêpes, put the flour, sugar and a pinch of salt in a large bowl. Make a well in the centre, add the eggs, oil and 2 tablespoons of the milk, and beat together with a wooden spoon until smooth. Slowly start to pour in a little milk, mixing as you pour, to keep the batter smooth. Pour in the rest of the milk, a bit more quickly now, until it looks like single cream. Finally, add the beer.
2 Heat a 15cm/6in crêpe pan and wipe the base with oiled kitchen paper. Measure 2½ tablespoons of the batter into a jug, then pour it into the pan, moving it around so the mixture swirls and covers the bottom of the pan. When the crêpe is golden underneath (in about 15 seconds if the pan is the right temperature), turn and cook for a further 30 seconds, until spotted brown.
3 Slide the crêpe onto a plate. Wipe the pan with oiled kitchen paper and continue frying until all the batter is used, stacking the crêpes on top of each other as you cook them. (You can freeze the pancakes at this stage, wrapped in cling film and foil.) Set aside, ready to reheat in the sauce.
4 For the sauce, heat the butter and sugar in a deep frying pan (about 25cm/10in in diameter) over a low heat, stirring occasionally, until the sugar begins to dissolve. Turn up the heat and bubble quite fast, until the mixture just starts to go brown and caramelise (about 4 minutes), stirring only towards the end. Pour in the orange juice, add the orange and lemon zests, letting the mixture bubble for 3–4 minutes to thicken slightly. Add the Grand Marnier and cognac, heat for a few seconds and lower the heat.
5 Put one crêpe into the juices and, holding it with a fork, coat it well in the mixture. Fold it into quarters and push to one side of the pan. Continue the coating and folding with the remaining crêpes. Serve 2–3 crêpes per person with the sauce.

Lemon Tart

I don't remember the first lemon tart I ever tasted, but I remember the most recent, and why I liked it so much. It was the last test of many in my search for the ultimate recipe for this exquisite dessert. The prototypes had received accolades, as well as criticisms, but this one, the result of much fine-tuning, was everything I wanted it to be. I began by canvassing some foodie friends to see what qualities they expected from a lemon tart. Passions ran high, their descriptions and droolings reflected mine, but I could see I had my work cut out in satisfying all those well-honed tastes. We all agreed on the pastry: it had to be 'thin and crisp', 'buttery', 'melt in the mouth', 'slightly sweet and almost shortbready'. The filling and topping were another matter. I could see the balance between sweetness and sharpness was going to be tricky, as was the texture, but the description I decided to work towards was 'not floppy, not stiff, but stands on its own when sliced'. The one that inspired me for the taste was that the tart should 'sing with the flavour of the best Italian lemons'. I gathered together all the recipes I could. Proportions of egg, sugar and lemon varied considerably, with some making a lemon curd-style filling by adding butter, a route I did not want to take. Those that added butter or lots of extra egg yolks I rejected, because the whole point of this tart is that it is light and not heavy and rich. Pastries ranged from straightforward shortcrust to fancy *pâtés sablées* and the tart's depth fluctuated from wafer thin to deeper than I cared to go. With all these ideas running round my head, I finally got cooking.

Perfecting the pastry

Pastry I know about. Or so I thought. I decided to start with a simple shortcrust pastry, but it lacked the shortbready crumbliness I was looking for. After my first attempt, I realised the pastry needed to be more buttery, sweeter (no sugar had been added), thinner and crumblier. On baking, I was also finding that the pastry (which had shrunk on cooking) was not crisp enough on the base and that the filling was pulling away from the edges. The depth of the tart also became an ongoing debate.

The filling – how lemony?

My instinctive balance of sugar, lemon and eggs worked well. 'Wow – it explodes in my mouth,' was one taster's comment. While some liked the texture of the lemon zest in the filling, others found it distracting. So, I strained out the zest but, not wanting to lose its sharpness, I let it infuse with the other ingredients while making the pastry. I decided the recipe was more accurate therefore worked better with a measurement

of lemon juice since, for the amount I required, the number of lemons needed varied enormously – from three to five, depending on how juicy they were.

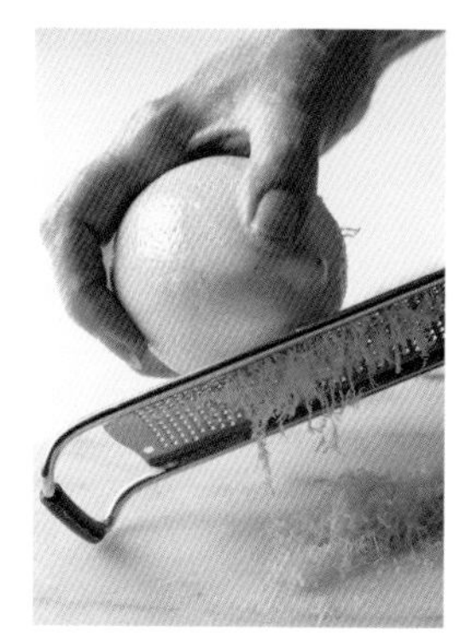

1 Finely grate the zest and make sure there is no pith.

Fine-tuning the details

Eventually the tart came out looking good but I learnt another lesson: you need to let it cool completely. After just 20 minutes, it was warm and tasted of lemon curd. The pastry was still not crisp on the bottom, so I tried baking it on a preheated baking sheet, and I wanted it thinner still. Bubbles were appearing on the surface, so, instead of using a whisk, I beat the filling with a wooden spoon.

The best topping

In my eagerness to sort out the pastry and filling I had paid no attention to the topping. I could just leave it bare as the silky smoothness was certainly attractive. I returned to my tasters. Some wanted it 'dusted with icing sugar, no other adornment', another fancied a 'crisp brûlée', while someone else wanted to see 'little bits of lemon rind on top'. A dusting of icing sugar did it for me, but I still liked the notion of breaking through a crisp brûlée into the velvet creaminess beneath. So here I offer both – a brûlée for those who have a blow torch, and icing sugar for those who do not.

2 Brûlée with a blow torch to caramelise the sugar for individual chef-style slices.

At last, a dream come true

Everything seemed in order until I tested the tart in a different oven. The filling was suddenly low in the pastry case and cracking like the Grand Canyon, and it had separated from the pastry again. The reasons? My original versions were baked in an electric oven, not a fan oven, and my filling was poured into a hot, not a cold, pastry case. Adapting the recipe for the fan oven closed the pastry cracks; a wider, shallower tin gave the right depth; and shrinkage was eliminated by having the pastry above the level of the tin before baking. The taste improved thanks to the fine-bladed Microplane grater. The zest glided off this like candy floss. My original tart had become far more alluring. I was delighted and so were my tasters.

Cuts into 12 elegant slices

Ready in 1½–1¾ hours

Fairly easy

What you need
For the pastry
100g/4oz cold butter, cut into chunks
175g/6oz plain flour
2 tbsp golden caster sugar
¼ tsp salt
1 egg yolk

For the filling
6 eggs, preferably organic
250g/9oz golden caster sugar
3–5 unwaxed lemons, finely grated zest of 3, juice of all (175ml/6fl oz strained juice)
150ml carton double cream
icing sugar, for sifting

The recipe

1 To make the pastry, rub the butter into the flour. Stir in the sugar and salt. Make a well in the flour, add the egg yolk and 1 tablespoon of cold water. Work into a dough; knead gently, adding a drop more water if needed. (Or make in the food processor.) Wrap in greaseproof paper. Chill for 20 minutes. Heat the oven to 190°C/fan 170°C/Gas 5 and put a baking sheet inside.

2 Meanwhile, make the filling. Use a wooden spoon to beat the eggs in a large bowl with the sugar until well blended, then stir in the lemon zest and juice. Leave to stand.

3 Roll out the pastry to fit a tart tin 24cm x 2cm/9½in x ¾in deep. Loosely line the tin with pastry, fitting it into the edges. Roll a rolling pin over the top to neaten the edge. Press into the flutes so the pastry is slightly above the tin. Prick the base lightly with a fork. Chill for 10 minutes.

4 Bake the pastry blind until set and pale golden, 12–15 minutes. Remove the beans and paper, and bake for a further 10–12 minutes until the base is cooked.

5 Meanwhile, strain the filling, skim off any surface froth and gently stir in the cream. Slowly pour into the case (if you have a sliding oven shelf, this can be done with the tart still on it). Reduce the heat to 150°C/fan 120°C/Gas 2. Bake until barely set, with a slight wobble in the centre, 30–35 minutes. Cool for at least 45 minutes. Serve the same day, with a light dusting of sifted icing sugar.

For a crisp brûlée topping
Dust the whole tart generously with sifted icing sugar and brûlée with a blow torch until starting to caramelise. Or, to serve individual slices, chef-style: slice, dust the slices generously with icing sugar, then brûlée each one individually.

Vanilla Ice Cream

I have to confess, I've never been a big ice-cream maker. There is a little machine tucked in the back of my kitchen cupboard that rarely gets an outing. Now I've finally seen the light. Homemade ice cream isn't as much trouble as you might think, and nothing beats the flavour and quality. If you're still in doubt, look at the number of ingredients in some commercial ice creams – I found up to 15. I already had so many eager tasters lining up in anticipation I was almost forcibly dispatched to the kitchen. I whipped up a batch to keep them at bay, then began the research. My aim was to create an ice cream that felt almost velvety smooth in the mouth, was creamy but not sickly, didn't taste overpoweringly of eggs or sugar, and had a gentle flavour of vanilla.

First the science bit

Although I only had four or five ingredients to worry about, the balance had to be right for both flavour and texture. This was where I needed help, chemistry not being my strong point. I knew just the person to quiz – Robin Weir, co-author of *Ices: the Definitive Guide* (Hodder and Stoughton) and a passionate authority on the subject. 'Unfortunately commercial ice cream is most people's idea of the norm. One of my aims in life is to get more people making their own,' said Robin. 'The sugar, apart from adding sweetness, stops ice cream from freezing solid like an ice cube,' he explained. 'The amount of fat dictates the richness of the ice cream, emulsifies the ingredients and has the effect of creating a smooth sensation in the mouth. The fat globules in milk and cream also inhibit the growth of large ice crystals. However, add too much fat and the ice cream will be dreadful – flaky in texture and unpleasant in taste. Mix in too much sugar and it will never freeze.' This was as much chemistry as I needed for now. I was ready to get testing.

Cream, milk or both?

In readiness for churning, ice cream machine canisters were put in the freezer overnight. You do need to think ahead, as the container needs to be super-cold before use (unless you have a deluxe machine with a built-in compressor which you just switch on and churn). The first decision was whether to use milk, cream or a mixture. Food writer Barney Desmazery recalled a Cornish chef telling him ice cream must be made purely with cream. The authenticity of it appealed, but the taste proved far too buttery. I then tried just milk, a favourite of Shona Crawford Poole, author of *Ice Cream* (Conran Octopus). 'It reminds me of the Italian ice cream I ate as a child,' said Shona. When I tried it, however,

I missed the creaminess, so I tried batches made with milk and single cream (still a bit thin-tasting) and milk and whipping cream (a bit lightweight). What I loved best was the creaminess of full-fat milk together with double cream – rich without tasting too fatty. However, other ingredients were now affecting the flavour and texture. I found six egg yolks to 700ml/1¼ pints of milk and cream combined gave an overeggy and sickly result. Four worked better. Trying to be health-conscious, I reduced the sugar, but got a firmer ice cream with less taste.

1 Scrape out the black seeds of the vanilla pod before adding the whole lot to the cream mixture.

Choosing the vanilla

No wonder vanilla's so expensive: it was originally an exotic perfume, first used to flavour ice cream in the early 1700s, Robin Weir told me. Which type – extract, bean or paste – would give the flavour I was after? Shona Crawford Poole favoured a good-quality extract, seeing the seeds from the bean as a fashion fad. Robin Weir made an interesting observation: 'Americans won't buy vanilla ice cream if it hasn't got the seeds in, whereas the British think they've got ice cream with specks of dust in it.' I tried vanilla extract, but even a good-quality one gave a commercial aftertaste. Vanilla paste (seeds suspended in a dark sugary syrup) marred the colour and taste. I much preferred the purity of the bean with its tiny seeds, but I wasn't getting enough flavour. I combined bean with a few drops of extract, but that spoilt the subtlety. To force out the flavour I zapped the whole bean in the blender with the sugar, Jamie Oliver-style, but the resulting ice cream looked grey and sooty. I then tried vanilla sugar plus a bean, but this was taking the vanilla taste too far. So I reduced the amount of all the ingredients slightly, kept the vanilla the same, and the flavour came bursting through.

2 The mixture should fall in thick ribbons when you lift the beaters.

Deciding on the method

I tried one non-custard-based recipe that involved neither cooking nor churning, more like a frozen, frothy, soft-scoop ice cream. Clever, but not for me. Most recipes tried to scare me off making the custard directly in the saucepan, as it can easily curdle, but as long as I used a good pan, kept the heat low, didn't let it boil, and kept stirring, all was fine.

To stir or to churn

Up until now I'd used an ice cream machine, but would it work as well by hand? I wouldn't be able to get in as much air without churning so I got air in another way, by whipping the cream. Though slightly less smooth, it still worked brilliantly. Robin Weir was right. He warned I'd become addicted to making my own ice cream, and I have.

3 Stir the custard all the time, until it is thick enough to coat the back of the spoon.

The recipe

Enough for 8 big scoops

Ready in 1¾–2 hours, plus overnight chilling and freezing

Fairly easy

What you need

284ml carton double cream
300ml/½ pint full-fat milk
115g/4oz golden caster sugar
1 vanilla pod
3 egg yolks, preferably organic
Have lots of ice at the ready

Can be frozen

How to make by hand
In step 1, heat the milk, vanilla, and half the sugar without the cream (the custard will be slightly thicker). At the start of step 6, whip the cream so it's light and floppy, not too stiff, and fold it into the cold custard. Freeze for 3–4 hours, stirring once an hour until almost frozen, then freeze as in recipe.

1 Put the canister from the machine into the freezer a day before you want to make the ice cream. Next day, pour the cream and milk into a medium heavy-based pan, then tip in half the sugar. Slit the vanilla pod down its length with a small sharp knife and scoop out as many of the tiny black seeds as you can into the cream mixture. Cut the pod into three and drop it into the pan.

2 Heat the cream and milk over a low heat, stirring occasionally, until it almost boils (you'll see a few bubbles at the edge). Take off the heat and set aside for 30 minutes so the vanilla can infuse.

3 Put the egg yolks into a bowl with the rest of the sugar and beat with an electric hand-beater for about 2 minutes until the mixture has thickened, is paler in colour and falls in thick ribbons when you lift the beaters. Using a measuring jug, scoop out about 125ml/4fl oz of the cream mixture and beat into the egg yolks to slacken them. Reheat the cream mix until it just comes to the boil, take off the heat and stir in the egg yolk mixture.

4 Return the pan to a low heat and cook, stirring all the time with a wooden spoon, for 8–10 minutes, until the custard is thick enough to coat the back of the spoon. Watch that it doesn't boil, as soon as you see any bubbles about to burst to the surface, it should be thick enough, so take the pan off the heat so the mixture doesn't curdle.

5 Pour the custard into a heatproof bowl, then sit it in a bigger bowl one-third full of iced water to cool (this takes about 20 minutes). Stir occasionally to stop a skin forming. Put the bowl of custard in the fridge for 3–4 hours, preferably overnight, so it gets really cold.

6 Get the ice cream machine running, scoop out the vanilla pod pieces, then slowly pour in the cold custard. Leave it to churn for 10–30 minutes (depending on your machine). When it stops, it will probably be too soft to eat, so spoon into a plastic container, cover with cling film, then a lid, and freeze for a minimum of 3 hours. (It will keep in the freezer for 3 months but don't take it out, then refreeze.) Remove from the freezer 15 minutes before serving.

Crème Brûlée

If there's one dessert worth getting fat for it's crème brûlée. I bet if you ask most people what is their favourite restaurant dessert, crème brûlée would come top of the list. So I knew I wouldn't be short of tasters, but I also knew expectations would be high. Collecting the ingredients gave me a sense of déjà vu, as they were the same as those I had used for vanilla ice cream. But what a different result I would get. For this recipe I had visions of achieving a glassy, smooth topping like a caramelised crust of thin ice which I could break through into a velvety custard – neither too thick nor too runny – a tricky texture to get just right. It was when I called Shaun Hill, award-winning chef, that the custard's consistency was clarified. 'It should be soft and unctuous,' he said, 'like a good mud.' Perfect, I thought.

The custardy layer

In all the recipes I researched, the ingredients varied little, but proportions did. A few used clotted cream, single or whipping cream, crème fraîche even, but the majority used just double cream. I tried this first, but found it a bit cloying. It was Shaun again who nudged me away from this. I tried using half milk, half cream, but found I had to add too many extra egg yolks to bump up the richness. Shaun recommended using a small amount of milk with double cream, which seemed to cut through the richness without compromising it. The texture was beautiful, too. So although I was early into my testing, I felt the custard was coming together. I wasn't going to question whether to use a vanilla pod over extract after all my experimenting with vanilla ice cream. A pod it was.

To bake or not to bake?

Crème brûlée can either be made on the stove then poured into dishes to set, baked in the oven, or done as a combination of the two. I found the oven version the most foolproof; the stove method required more skill for the mixture not to curdle and be thick enough to set, while the combination seemed overcomplicated. I tried different oven temperatures and timings and liked the result a medium-low oven gave me. It was now time to choose a dish. I had two options: ramekins or wider shallower dishes. 'It all depends on how you like the ratio of custard to caramel,' advised Shaun. I decided to opt for ramekins, preferring the depth they gave to the custard layer.

Cracking the crust

Topping possibilities now lay before me. Shaun advised, 'Caster sugar is better. I don't like too much, I think it's there to set off the custard, so one layer is enough for me.' I recalled a recipe of Gary Rhodes, where he builds up several layers with icing sugar. Others favoured demerara sugar, and in *Delia Smith's Complete Illustrated Cookery Course* (BBC Books), she pours caramel over, 'to help those who (like me) have never had a domestic grill that is suitable for fast caramelising of sugar.' I tried the lot, but I wasn't getting my glassy layer. I called food writer Anne Willan in France as she, too, has done a lot of research on this recipe. She sent me one that she found in *The Experienced English Housekeeper* by Elizabeth Raffald, dated 1769. It said the topping should 'look like a glass plate put over the cream.' Exactly, but how to achieve it?

Time to get picky

The tasters' enthusiasm wasn't flagging, and they were happy with the results but I knew I hadn't reached the ultimate yet, as small details were niggling me. Although the custard was now a lovely consistency in the centre, the edges had a slightly overcooked, scrambled look. What was causing that? I was getting a skin on the custard so it would support the brûlée layer, but it was too brown. I reminded myself that this is a restaurant dish; I needed to visit a friendly chef.

Last minute tips and tweaks

Lawrence Keogh, head chef at West Street Restaurant in London and his pastry chef, Julien Philippe, treated me to a demonstration. It was their helpful tips that turned my recipe around. A chance remark from Julien about putting a baking sheet over the ramekins while they bake intrigued me. Could this solve the problem of the overcooked edges and brown tops? I tried it later, and the custard was transformed. I followed Julien's advice on filling the ramekins right to the top and found it gave a better surface for the brûlée. The best tip, however, was from Lawrence, who suggested spraying a fine film of water over the sugar. This dissolves it slightly before it gets zapped with the blow torch. And yes, a blow torch does do the best job, so is worth investing in (grilling, I found, overcooked the custard). As my spoon cracked its way through the golden glassy topping, it slid into a velvety pool of lusciousness. 'Calories?' I thought. 'What are they?'

1 Slice the vanilla pod in half lengthways to scrape out the seeds.

2 Spread the sugar with the back of a spoon to give an even covering.

3 Dampen the sugar with a fine spray of water.

4 Keep moving the blow torch round to evenly colour the top.

The recipe

Serves 4

Ready in 1¼–1½ hours, plus several hours or overnight chilling

Fairly easy

What you need

2 cartons double cream, 1 large (284ml) plus 1 small (142ml)
100ml/3½fl oz full-fat milk
1 vanilla pod
5 egg yolks, preferably organic
50g/2oz golden caster sugar, plus extra for the topping

1 Heat the oven to 180°C/fan 160°C/Gas 4. Sit four 175ml/6fl oz ramekins in a deep roasting tin at least 7.5cm/3in deep (or a large deep cake tin), one that will enable a baking tray to sit well above the ramekins when laid across the top of the tin. Pour the two cartons of cream into a medium pan with the milk. Lay the vanilla pod on a board and slice it lengthways through the middle with a sharp knife to split it in two. Use the tip of the knife to scrape out all the tiny seeds into the cream mixture. Drop the vanilla pod in as well, and set aside.

2 Put the egg yolks and sugar in a mixing bowl and whisk for 1 minute with an electric hand-whisk until paler in colour and a bit fluffy. Put the pan with the cream on a medium heat and bring almost to the boil. As soon as you see bubbles appear round the edge, take the pan off the heat.

3 Pour the hot cream into the beaten egg yolks, stirring with a wire whisk as you do so, and scraping out the seeds from the pan. Set a fine sieve over a large wide jug or bowl and pour the hot mixture through to strain it, encouraging any stray vanilla seeds through at the end. Using a big spoon, scoop off all the pale foam that is sitting on the top of the liquid (this will be several spoonfuls) and discard. Give the mixture a stir.

4 Pour in enough hot water (from the tap is fine) into the roasting tin to come about 1.5cm/⅝in up the sides of the ramekins. Pour the hot cream into the ramekins so you fill them up right to the top (it's easier to spoon in the last little bit). Put them in the oven and lay a baking sheet over the top of the tin so it sits well above the ramekins and completely covers them, but not the whole tin, leaving a small gap at one side to allow air to circulate. Bake for 30–35 minutes until the mixture is softly set. To check, gently sway the roasting tin and if the crème brûlées are ready, they will wobble a bit like a jelly in the middle. Don't let them get too firm.

5 Lift the ramekins out of the roasting tin with oven gloves and set them on a wire rack to cool for a couple of minutes only, then put in the fridge to cool completely. This can be done overnight without affecting the texture.

6 When ready to serve, wipe round the top edge of the dishes, sprinkle 1½ teaspoons of caster sugar over each ramekin and spread it out with the back of a spoon to completely cover (Anne Willan's tip for an even layer). Spray with a little water using a fine spray (the sort you buy in a craft shop) to just dampen the sugar, then use a blow torch to caramelise it. Hold the flame just above the sugar and keep moving it round and round until caramelised. Serve when the brûlée is firm, or within an hour or two.

Apple Pie

The ultimate apple pie is a rare thing. I'd tasted it once at Ballymaloe, Darina Allen's cookery school in Ireland. Everything worked together beautifully; the buttery pastry caressed a pure, fruity filling, undistorted by too many other flavours. However, my first test, using a well-used classic recipe, was bland. The pastry was rubbed in with half fat (not all butter) to flour and the apples were Bramleys drizzled with lemon, but when I cut it, out rushed a torrent of thin juices. Then there was the gaping void left between the filling and pastry. Why was that?

Seeking advice

I called Darina Allen at Ballymaloe and it was clear that her recipe relied on access to the best ingredients – apples fresh from the tree – and her mother's unusual pastry recipe. Darina gave me food for thought, but I knew I needed to come up with my own version, so continued my search by concentrating on the pastry.

Perking up the pastry

Not wanting to give up on the traditional 'rubbing-in' method, I did various tests. I definitely preferred an all-butter version, and was now adding more than half butter to flour for better flavour and texture. I then tried Darina's recipe and loved how it hugged the apples as the pie baked, eliminating that big void. The pastry method was new to me – made with eggs and by 'creaming' the fat – more like making a cake than pastry. However, I found the result a bit too cakey, so reduced the egg and ended up with a hybrid of the best elements from both Darina's and the 'rubbed in' all-butter version.

Choosing the perfect apples

As the geographical origins of apple pie are hazy, I quizzed international food writers for their favoured apple. I sensed Bramleys would be best, and food writer Ruth Watson agreed. 'I like the way they behave,' she told me. Not having easy access to cooking apples, food writer Susan Spungen, in the US, mixes two eating varieties: 'one that will cook into silky slices which hold their shape well like a Granny Smith, and one that will break down into apple sauce, like MacIntosh, to hold it together.' Food writer Anne Willan, in France, said: 'It must be a tart apple that holds some shape when cooked.' I tried all sorts of combinations but followed Ruth Watson's maxim that simplicity must be the key, and as Bramleys were providing the texture and flavour I was after, went just for these, discarding unnecessary flavourings such as

orange zest. Ruth also encouraged me to be less mean with the filling. 'I like pies to look all lumpy in a volcanic way, all humped up and gorgeous,' she said. So that's how I did mine, and it did look gorgeous.

Last-minute revelation

I still hadn't eliminated the runny juice from the filling. I then remembered a North American trick I had used before, of tossing the apples in a mix of sugar and flour. This helped but was still not enough. Then the answer suddenly came while working with Gordon Ramsay one day as he prepared a pear dessert. He let the peeled pears stand for over half an hour. Since they were turning brown, I asked why he hadn't doused them in lemon juice. He said he wanted them to discolour, as exposure to the air drew out the moisture and concentrated the flavour. Could this work with apples? I rushed back to the kitchen, sliced the apples and, against my better judgment, let them go brown while the pastry chilled. Miraculously, with my flour/sugar mix and browned apples, I ended up with a beautifully cooked filling of apples (for some reason no longer brown) enclosed in a syrupy sauce, lying snugly under their perfect pastry duvet. Delicious!

1 Cover the apple slices with kitchen paper and set aside so they discolour.

2 Pile the apples high in the pastry-lined tin.

3 Cover the apples with a pastry lid and trim the edge with a sharp knife.

The recipe

Serves 8

Ready in 2¼–2½ hours, including chilling and baking

Fairly easy

What you need
For the filling
1kg/2lb 4oz Bramley apples
140g/5oz golden caster sugar
½ tsp cinnamon
3 tbsp plain flour

For the pastry
225g/8oz butter, room temperature
50g/2oz golden caster sugar, plus extra
2 eggs
350g/12oz plain flour, preferably organic
softly whipped cream, to serve

Can be frozen (unbaked)

1 Put a layer of kitchen paper on a large baking sheet. Quarter, core, peel and slice the apples about 5mm/¼in thick and lay evenly on the baking sheet. Put kitchen paper on top and set aside while you make and chill the pastry.
2 For the pastry, beat the butter and 50g/2oz sugar in a large bowl until just mixed. Break in a whole egg and a yolk (keep the white for glazing later). Beat together for just under 1 minute (it will look a bit like scrambled egg). Now work in the flour with a wooden spoon, a third at a time, until it's beginning to clump up, then finish gathering it together with your hands. Gently work the dough into a ball, wrap in cling film, and chill for 45 minutes. Now mix the 140g/5oz sugar, the cinnamon and flour for the filling in a bowl that is large enough to take the apples later.
3 After the pastry has chilled, heat the oven to 190°C/fan 170°C/Gas 5. Lightly beat the egg white with a fork. Cut off a third of the pastry and keep it wrapped while you roll out the rest, and use this to line a pie tin (20–22cm/8–8½in round and 4cm/1½in deep) leaving a slight overhang. Roll the remaining third to a circle about 28cm/11in in diameter. Pat the apples dry with kitchen paper, and tip them into the bowl with the cinnamon-sugar mix. Give a quick mix with your hands and immediately pile the apples high into the pastry-lined tin.
4 Brush a little water around the pastry rim and lay the pastry lid over the apples, pressing the edges together to seal. Trim the edge with a sharp knife and make 5 little slashes on top of the lid for the steam to escape. (Can be frozen at this stage.) Brush it all with the egg white and sprinkle with caster sugar. Bake for 40–45 minutes, until golden, then remove and let it sit for 5–10 minutes. Sprinkle with more sugar and serve while still warm from the oven with softly whipped cream.

Sticky Toffee Pudding

A lot of puddings are naughty but sticky toffee pudding has to be the naughtiest. 'It's a pudding that's about excess,' Sophie Grigson told me. 'The best one I've eaten had a huge puddle of sauce and custard too.' This decadent dessert was created by Francis Coulson, one of the founders of the Sharrow Bay Country House Hotel in the Lake District. According to Layla Denwood, one of their pastry chefs, it is their best-selling pudding, still made to the original recipe.

Not sticky enough

Though I found that ingredients varied little in most recipes, amounts and methods did. I knew what I was after. First and foremost was stickiness. 'It has to be moist, but not wet-moist, and both sticky and soft, light but not too light,' Sophie said. My first test was definitely not a contender. I loved its simplicity, the dates weren't soaked and it was made like a simple cake mix with boiling water stirred in at the end. However, it was like a tasteless, dense sponge with a few sunken chopped dates dropped in. I decided to reduce the flour and eggs and change the type of sugar. Also, I'd made one big pudding, and the servings looked hefty. Mark Hix at The Ivy showed me his version done in individual pudding tins. They looked much daintier.

Reworking the recipe

Boiling water was providing lightness, but instead of pouring it in neat, I used it to soak the dates. This created a purée that improved the pudding's texture and allowed the dates to blend in better. I tried losing the bicarbonate of soda, but Layla told me it was essential. 'It makes the puddings lighter and airier.' I had used light muscovado sugar thinking that would provide the toffee taste and colour but it hadn't. I tried mixing light and dark muscovado but that wasn't quite right either. Remembering how the caramel taste of demerara sugar had turned my flapjack recipe around (see page 144), I tried that, and for depth of colour, taste and gooey texture, stirred in two spoonfuls of black treacle. This was more like it – moist, light, sticky and soft all in one mouthful.

Keeping it saucy

The simplest sauce I made was by heating sugar, butter and cream in a pan until combined. It was fine, but dulled on cooling and was a bit grainy. I found by boiling the sugar, butter and some of the cream (as they do at The Ivy) then stirring in the rest of the cream, the sauce was far glossier, smoother and toffee-like, especially when I added black treacle.

Layla Denwood shared a final tip. 'We keep the puddings covered in the sauce for two days, so it soaks in.' Not only did they remain light, they went even stickier. As I scraped the last mouthful from my plate I recalled Sophie Grigson saying, 'this pudding is like all good parties – one should leave wanting slightly more.' Seconds anyone?

The recipe

Makes 7 little puddings

Ready in about 1½ hours (best made a day or two ahead and left to soak up the sauce, see recipe)

Easy

What you need
For the puddings
225g/8oz whole dates
175ml/6fl oz boiling water
1 tsp vanilla extract
2 eggs
175g/6oz self-raising flour
1 tsp bicarbonate of soda
85g/3oz butter, softened
140g/5oz demerara sugar
2 tbsp black treacle
100ml/3½fl oz milk
cream or custard to serve, but only if you feel the need

For the toffee sauce
175g/6oz light muscovado sugar
50g/2oz butter, cut into pieces
225ml/8fl oz double cream
1 tbsp black treacle

Can be frozen (Freeze any spare puddings in an oven-proof dish with some of the sauce for later. Thaw for a few hours and reheat as per recipe method.)

1 Stone and chop the dates quite small, put them in a bowl and pour the boiling water over. Leave for about half an hour until cool and well soaked, then mash a bit with a fork and stir in the vanilla. Butter and flour 7 mini pudding tins (each about 200ml/7fl oz) and sit them on a baking sheet. Heat the oven to 180°C/fan 160°C/Gas 4.

2 Meanwhile, make the puddings. Beat the eggs. Mix the flour and bicarbonate of soda together. Beat the butter and sugar together with an electric hand-mixer for a couple of minutes, until slightly creamy (mixture will be grainy from the sugar). Add the eggs a little at a time, beating well between each addition. Beat in the black treacle. Using a large metal spoon, gently fold in one third of the flour then half the milk, being careful not to overbeat. Repeat until all the flour and milk are used. Stir the soaked dates into the pudding batter. The mix will look curdled at this point, and be like a soft, thick batter. Spoon it evenly between the pudding tins. Bake for 20–25 minutes until risen and firm.

3 While the puddings bake, make the sauce. Put the sugar and butter in a medium saucepan with half the cream. Bring to the boil over a medium heat, stirring all the time, until the sugar has completely dissolved. Stir in the black treacle, then let the mixture bubble away for 2–3 minutes until it is a rich toffee colour, stirring occasionally to make sure it doesn't burn. Take the pan off the heat and beat in the rest of the cream.

4 When the puddings are done, take them out of the oven. Leave in the tins for a few minutes then loosen them well from the sides of the tins with a small palette knife before turning them out. You can serve them now, but they'll be even stickier if left for a day or two coated in the sauce. To do this, pour about half the sauce into one or two ovenproof serving dishes (whatever you have that is big enough to take all the puddings). Sit the upturned puddings on the sauce, then pour the rest of it over. Cover with a loose tent of foil so the sauce doesn't get smudged.

5 When ready to serve, heat the oven to 180°C/fan 160°C/Gas 4. Warm the puddings through, still covered, for 15–20 minutes or until the sauce is bubbly. Serve as is, or with cream or custard.

Summer Pudding

I've always wanted to like summer pudding more than I actually have. I love the blend of the juicy summer fruits that make up this very British pudding, but the problem for me has always been that outer casing of patchy pink, usually soggy, often collapsing layer of bread. Like many people I know, I often push it to the edge of the plate and just enjoy the fruit. This recipe was going to be a challenge: getting the right blend of fruits was crucial, but most important would be a happy intermingling of the fruit and bread. Before I began, a quick chat with Sophie Grigson got me focused. 'I still use my mother's recipe,' said Sophie. 'It must have blackcurrants for a good backdrop flavour, and I hate cooked strawberries in it.'

The right balance of fruit

I found recipes using cherries, gooseberries, plums and even rhubarb, combined with the more traditional raspberries and currants. This seemed odd. I couldn't think of even a week when all these fruits would be in season at the same time. I opted for high summer fruits: strawberries, raspberries and British currants. Like Sophie Grigson, I am not keen on cooked strawberries, but they won in the end when I let them steep rather than cook in the syrup; the fruity mixture benefited from their sweet flavour, shape and texture. Raspberries and redcurrants have good setting qualities, so would help make a pudding with substance.

A chance discovery

For the filling, most recipes call for simmering the sugar, water and fruit for about five minutes. Sounds easy, but I ended up with too much watery liquid and fruit that had lost its charm. I decided to make a syrup, then add the fruit in stages. While the sugar was dissolving in the water and cassis (added for extra depth), I was distracted by the phone. On returning to the pan, my simple syrup was about to turn to caramel. Not wishing to waste it, I threw in the currants, stirred and let it gently bubble for no more than a minute, just to soften the fruit. The end result was rich, almost jammy. Wanting to keep the integrity of the raspberries and strawberries, I let the syrup cool right down before adding them.

The right bread is key

Instinctively I felt the best choice would be a good farmhouse white that I could slice myself to just the right thickness. I tried brioche, but found its sweetness rather cloying. After trying several other loaves

(cheap sliced white was the least favourite, far too damp and squidgy) I found my instinct was right. Fresh farmhouse loaf was fine, but leaving it for 2–3 days to go stale created just the right texture and absorbency.

Yet another discovery

After initially lining the basin with the bread, then watching the pudding slowly collapse after it was turned out, I tried layering the bread and fruit. I was thrilled with the result. The bread no longer dominated; it complemented the fruit and absorbed the juices without going soggy. It turned out more easily, and even more remarkable, it stayed upright for hours. Until I stumbled across this different presentation, I was always disappointed after turning out the classic version. You couldn't see the fruit, and I would desperately try to perk up its looks before carrying it to the table. Now, I have to do nothing. It looks fantastic just as it is.

1 Run a fork down the length of each stem to remove the currants.

2 Gently stir the fruits with a large metal spoon so that they don't break up.

3 Layer the bread and fruit. Finish with a final layer of bread and press it down.

The recipe

Serves 6

Ready in
1 hour 20 minutes–1½ hours, plus overnight chilling

Easy

What you need
1.15kg/2lb 8oz mixture of British summer fruits (I liked the combination of 350g/12oz raspberries, 350g/12oz small strawberries, 300g/10oz blackcurrants, 175g/6oz redcurrants, but this is not definitive – experiment with your own blend and try mixing in loganberries and tayberries)
175g/6oz golden caster sugar
5 tbsp crème de cassis (blackcurrant liqueur) or crème de mûre (blackberry liqueur)
2–3-day-old small unsliced farmhouse white loaf (you will need about 5 slices)
double cream, to serve

Can be frozen

1 First get all the fruit ready. Hull the strawberries and cut them in halves or quarters depending on how big they are. Strip the blackcurrants and redcurrants from their stalks in one fell swoop by running a fork down the length of each stem. Keep both the currants separate from the other fruits.
2 Tip the sugar into a wide, not too deep, saucepan. Measure in 3 tablespoons water and the cassis. Put the pan on a low heat and cook, stirring often, until you can no longer hear the crunch of sugar grains on the bottom of the pan. When the sugar is dissolved, turn up the heat to medium-high and let the mixture bubble away for about 8 minutes. It will go quite syrupy and you want to catch it just before it starts to change colour or caramelise.
3 Now tip the blackcurrants and redcurrants into the hot syrup, it will feel quite sticky at first, then bring everything back up to a lively simmer and let it bubble again for no more than a minute, just to lightly burst and soften the currants without losing their shape. Take the pan off the heat and leave until the fruit mixture is barely warm.
4 Gently stir in the strawberries and raspberries (a large metal spoon is best so they don't break up) and let the fruity mixture sit for about half an hour so the juices all mix in.
5 Cut 4–5 slices from the loaf, about 5mm/¼in thick, and trim off the crusts. Cut a little square (about 4cm) from one slice and put it in the bottom of a 1.2 litre/2 pint pudding basin. Using a big slotted spoon, put a layer of fruit (about 3 spoonfuls) over the bread. Next lay a slice of bread in the centre over the fruit, trimming to fit and fill any gaps with trimmings of bread so the fruit is covered. Continue layering with more fruit, more bread, then a final layer of fruit so it comes to within a hair's breadth of the top of the basin. Spoon over a few spoonfuls of juice – not too much or it will ooze out when weighted down. (You should have about 4 spoonfuls of fruit and juice left for making a sauce.) Cover the fruit with a final layer of bread, press down to compact everything, then cover with cling film. Lay a saucer on top and weight down with heavy cans or weights. Stand the basin on a plate in case any juices spill out, then leave in the fridge overnight, or for a minimum of 5 hours. Press the leftover fruits and juice through a metal sieve to make a sauce, and keep chilled. (You can freeze the pudding and the sauce at this stage for up to a month.)
6 To turn out, go round the edge of the pudding with a round-bladed knife to release it, then invert it onto a plate. Cut into slices with a serrated knife and serve with a drizzle of the fruit sauce and cream.

Lemon Meringue Pie

When it I was little, the way I made lemon meringue pie was by tipping a packet of powdery filling into a pan, mixing it with water and waiting for the lemon flavour to burst out of a tiny pill-like capsule as it dissolved. Looking at the ingredients listed on the packet now, I discover the yellow colour comes not from fresh lemons and brilliant yellow egg yolks but turmeric! No wonder I wanted to make one with a more sophisticated taste.

Tackling the recipe

I started at the bottom, making the pastry in the food processor for ease, enriching it with egg yolk and butter for a crisp and buttery finish. After testing a few versions made with the classic custard-type filling of varying amounts of cornflour, sugar, egg yolks, lemon juice and zest and around 300ml/½ pint water, I was even more determined to update this dessert. Why use so much water? No taste or flavour was going in, just volume. To create a softer, richer filling that was more of a cross between lemon curd and lemon tart, instinct told me to add more egg, some butter and less cornflour and water.

A filling full of flavour

I turned to a Jane Grigson recipe and was amazed to see her filling was a lemon-curd lookalike. It was delicious, but very high in sugar and butter, and far richer than the classic. I returned to using cornflour and water, but tried to add more flavour. One solution came from Phil Vickery, a great pudding maker. He told me he uses a recipe given to him by Brian Gilham, an old college lecturer, who was pastry chef to the Queen for 16 years. He makes the water up with lemon barley water, adding more lemon juice and zest than normal, making the filling incredibly lemony. If you like real tartness, it's great, but a bit too mouth-puckering for me. Knowing how popular lemon meringue pie is in the US, I visited former Harrods' executive pastry chef, Bill McCarrick, an American. He suggested mixing orange juice with the water, 'it will add subtle colour and flavour without taking over from the lemon.' It did just that. I was now using less cornflour and liquid, so to counteract this I added a whole egg as well as yolks as thickener which, along with the extra butter, gave a silkier texture. Cooking the eggs a bit in the filling before pouring it into the pastry case, which most recipes don't do, thickened it to give a more stable surface for the meringue to sit on.

Topping it off

Time to tackle the meringue. This is where a lot of weeping, slipping and sliding can happen. Mary Berry shared her favourite tip: 'Choose a very big bowl for whisking the whites, then move both the bowl and the beater so you get lots of air in.' A classic meringue uses twice as much sugar to egg whites, but when used as a topping, it often works in reverse. Bill McCarrick favours the classic recipe with all caster sugar; Mary Berry uses less; Phil Vickery combines icing sugar and caster and bakes it in a very hot oven for 4–5 minutes. Mary Berry bakes hers for 45 minutes in a very low oven. However, after trying more and less sugar, high and low oven temperatures, I still hadn't resolved the problem of 'weeping'.

1 Stir the filling constantly until it is thickened and smooth.

The magic of meringues

I referred to the American cooking bible *Joy of Cooking* (Simon & Schuster, USA). The authors' logical explanation is that if the meringue goes on a cold filling, it never gets cooked properly. They write: 'The undercooked part of the meringue simply melts as the pie stands, resulting in that infamous slippery puddle between filling and topping.' Their solution is to have the filling hot as the meringue goes on, so the underneath part has a chance to cook as it hits the lemony layer. This made sense and the addition of cornflour gave me a more stable meringue that was crisp on the outside, marshmallowy within. I cooked it for 20 minutes at a medium heat, and found that if I let the pie stand for about an hour, it enabled the filling to settle and cut perfectly.

2 Pour the reheated filling into the pastry case.

Last-minute adjustments

Now all I had to decide was how to serve the pie. All of my culinary advisers agreed that it must be served at room temperature, and on the day it is made. However, I did have a slice left over the next day and the pastry and meringue remained crisp, without a puddle in sight. That packet of lemon meringue pie-filling will never get a look in again.

3 Spoon on the meringue starting from the edge.

The recipe

Serves 6–8

Ready in 1½–1¾ hours from start to finish, 40–50 mins if you make and bake the pastry a day ahead

Fairly easy

What you need
For the pastry
175g/6oz plain flour
100g/4oz cold butter, cut into small pieces
1 tbsp icing sugar
1 egg yolk

For the filling
2 level tbsp cornflour
100g/4oz golden caster sugar
finely grated zest 2 large lemons
125ml/4fl oz fresh lemon juice (from 2–3 lemons)
juice 1 small orange
85g/3oz butter, cut into pieces
3 egg yolks and 1 whole egg

For the meringue
4 egg whites, room temperature
200g/8oz golden caster sugar
2 level tsp cornflour

1. For the pastry, put the flour, butter, icing sugar, egg yolk (save the white for the meringue) and 1 tablespoon cold water into a food processor. Using the pulse button so the mix is not overworked, process until the mix starts to bind. Tip the pastry onto a lightly floured surface, gather together until smooth, then roll out and line a 23cm x 2.5cm/9in x 1in loose-bottom fluted flan tin. Trim and neaten the edges. Press the pastry into the flutes. The pastry is quite rich, so don't worry if it cracks, just press it back together. Prick the base with a fork, line with foil, shiny side down, and chill for ½–1 hour (or overnight).
2. Put a baking sheet in the oven and heat the oven to 200°C/fan 180°C/Gas 6. Bake the pastry case 'blind' (filled with dry beans) for 15 minutes, then remove the foil and bake a further 5–8 minutes until the pastry is pale golden and cooked. Set aside. (This can be done a day ahead.) Lower the oven to 180°C/fan 160°C/Gas 4.
3. While the pastry bakes, prepare the filling: mix the cornflour, sugar and lemon zest in a medium saucepan. Strain and stir in the lemon juice gradually. Make the orange juice up to 200ml/7fl oz with water and strain into the pan. Cook over a medium heat, stirring constantly, until thickened and smooth. Once the mixture bubbles, remove from the heat and beat in the butter until melted. Beat the egg yolks (save whites for meringue) and the whole egg together, stir into the pan and return to a medium heat. Keep stirring vigorously for a few minutes, until the mixture thickens and plops from the spoon. (It will bubble, but doesn't curdle.) Take off the heat and set aside while you make the meringue.
4. Put the 4 saved egg whites in a large bowl. Whisk to soft peaks, then add half the sugar a spoonful at a time, whisking between each addition without overbeating. Whisk in the cornflour, then add the rest of the sugar as before until smooth and thick. Quickly reheat the filling and pour it into the pastry case. Immediately put spoonfuls of meringue around the edge of the filling (if you start in the middle the meringue may sink), then spread so it just touches the pastry (this will anchor it and help stop it sliding). Pile the rest into the centre, spreading so it touches the surface of the hot filling (and starts to cook), then give it all a swirl. Return to the oven for 18–20 minutes until the meringue is crisp and slightly coloured. Let the pie sit in the tin for 30 minutes, then remove and leave for at least another ½–1 hour before slicing. Eat the same day.

Information for using the recipes

The ingredients you need are fully described and explained throughout the book so I hope you will find everything clear and easy to follow. Where possible, use organic ingredients, humanely-reared meats, organic chickens and eggs, fish from a sustainable source and unrefined sugar. It is advisable to wash all fresh produce before preparation.

APPROXIMATE WEIGHT CONVERSIONS

- All the recipes in this book list both imperial and metric measurements. Conversions are approximate and have been rounded up or down. Follow one set of measurements only; do not mix the two.
- Conversions vary slightly in some recipes (e.g. 100g = 4oz or 115g = 4oz) because they work better with that particular metric amount.
- Cup measurements, which are used by cooks in Australia and America, have not been listed here as they vary from ingredient to ingredient. If you are used to cups, use kitchen scales instead to measure dry/solid ingredients.
- All eggs used in the recipes are large in the UK and Australia, unless otherwise stated. (American cooks please note that your 'extra large' eggs are the same size as the ones called 'large' in the UK.)

OVEN TEMPERATURES

Gas	°C	Fan °C	°F	Oven temp.
¼	110	90	225	Very cool
½	120	100	250	Very cool
1	140	120	275	Cool or slow
2	150	130	300	Cool or slow
3	160	140	325	Warm
4	180	160	350	Moderate
5	190	170	375	Moderately hot
6	200	180	400	Fairly hot
7	220	200	425	Hot
8	230	210	450	Very hot
9	240	220	475	Very hot

SPOON MEASURES

- Spoon measurements are level unless otherwise stated, using proper measuring spoons.
- 1 teaspoon = 5ml
- 1 tablespoon = 15ml

Australian cooks

Your tablespoons measure 20ml (4 teaspoons) whereas UK ones are only 15ml (3 teaspoons), so where tablespoons are given, please measure 3 teaspoons to get the correct amount.

APPROXIMATE LIQUID CONVERSIONS

metric	imperial	AUS	US
50ml	2fl oz	¼ cup	¼ cup
125ml	4fl oz	½ cup	½ cup
175ml	6fl oz	¾ cup	¾ cup
225ml	8fl oz	1 cup	1 cup
300ml	10fl oz/½ pint	½ pint	1¼ cups
450ml	16fl oz	2 cups	2 cups/1 pint
600ml	20fl oz/1 pint	1 pint	2½ cups
1 litre	35fl oz/1¾ pints	1¾ pints	1 quart

American cooks

Your pints are smaller – only 450ml whereas ours are 600ml. So for liquid measurements please use a British pint measure or follow the metric quantities given.

Index

Page numbers in italics indicate illustrations
Recipe names in bold type are for quick page reference

Acknowledgements

I would like to thank the following chefs, food writers and experts who have so generously shared their time and expertise during my search for the Ultimate recipes. Without their culinary insights and input this book could not have been written:

Darina Allen
Val Barrett
Ghillie Başan
Mary Berry
Vatcharin Bhumichitr
Alan Bird
Raymond Blanc
Charles Burton
Michael Caines
Robert Carrier
Sally Clarke
Gennaro Contaldo
Andy Cook
Shona Crawford Poole
Regis Crepy
Layla Denwood
Barney Desmazery
Tom Dolby
Ursula Ferrigno
Moyra Fraser
Stuart Gillies
Bill Granger
Sophie Grigson
Lulu Grimes
Roopa Gulati
Valentina Harris
Diana Henry
Shaun Hill
Mark Hix
Geraldene Holt
Ken Hom
Sara Jayne-Stanes
Stephen Jackson
Jennifer Joyce
Lawrence Keogh
Tom Kime
Atul Kochhar
Sue Lawrence
Dan Lepard
M. Alain Lhermitte
Lori Longbotham
Alex Mackay
Bill McCarrick
Umberto Menghi
Marie-Pierre Moine
Joyce Molyneux
Jean Christophe Novelli
Stephen Odlum
Namita Panjabi
Meena Pathak
Marguerite Patten
Julian Philippe
Kathryn Race
Gordon Ramsay
Gary Rhodes
Claudia Roden
Susan Spungen
Rick Stein
Ian Thomason
David Thompson
Mitch Tonks
Brian Turner
Anna Venturi
Phil Vickery
Marcus Wareing
Ruth Watson
Robin Weir
Jasper White
Anne Willan
Jeni Wright

To all the authors (past and present) whose books I referred to, especially Elizabeth David, Jane Grigson, Delia Smith, Alice Waters and the authors of *Joy of Cooking* (Simon & Schuster, US).

Many thanks also to Simon Wheeler for his skillful photography and all his support during it, to Gillian Carter and those at *BBC Good Food Magazine*, as well as the many friends who have so willingly debated and tasted the Ultimate recipes, to Nigel Soper for stylishly designing the book and to all at BBC Books, especially Vivien Bowler and Dee O'Reilly, for turning a dream into a reality.